Are You
Buying This?

Praise for *Are You Buying This?*

"J. J. Robertson is like America's bartender: she hears our stories and sees our contradictions. And like a good bartender, she tells a great story and is funny as hell."

—**Greg Rice**, Managing Director, Kelton LA

"It's a much funnier, charming and useful US Census, and it's $13 billion cheaper!"

—**Darren Moran**, Founder of Creative Studio,
Gotham Bacon Concern

"Robertson has done the hard work of identifying the needs and wants of Americans, so you can better understand this country and its people. Mercifully for creative types, she leaves an abundance of statistics off the page leaving useful, often hilarious, insights."

—**Xanthe Wells**, Chief Creative Officer, Pitch

"This wildly original approach to understanding how and why consumers connect with brands is essential reading for anybody in sales. I'm not kidding."

—**John Karem**, VP Sales, Stoli Group

"*Are You Buying This?* just bumped *Hey Whipple, Squeeze This* from the top spot on my required reading list for aspiring advertising professionals."

—**Mike Wolfsohn**, Chief Creative Officer, High Wide & Handsome

"In a world where 'the marketing-jargon in the air is thicker than Beijing's smog,' *Are You Buying This?* offers us a clear and refreshing perspective on Americans and their relationship to living the dream."

—**Alasdair Lloyd-Jones**, President & CSO,
SET - A World Class Brand Experience Agency

"The only tears I cried were . . . tears of joy. Truths discovered in this delightful book made me laugh and think about how I can use them to grow our business."

—**Kim Haskell**, Partner, Phelps

"*Are You Buying This?* provides wonderfully informative answers on matters large and small that every marketer can take advantage of."

—**John Truscott**, President, High Wide & Handsome

"This smart, funny tour into the world of an account planner shines light on how advertisers connect with consumers in calculated and often hilarious ways."

—**Brian Creech**, Head of Production, Running With Scissors, The Martin Agency

"Whip smart. Insightful. Cheeky. Human. Fill out the Brain Fuel. Try the Field Work. Read the endnotes . . . a fascinating look at understanding who we are."

—**Denise Zurilgen**, Associate Creative Director, Droga5

"The advertising landscape can be a daunting battleground to navigate and I've always considered Robertson's perspective to be a cherished secret weapon. In *Are You Buying This?* her secrets come out of the bag. That's a great thing for all of us in this mad industry."

—**Tom Gilmartin**, Lead, Creative Shop, Facebook & Instagram

"*Are You Buying This?* is a delicious peek into what fascinates account planners. It will make you laugh out loud."

—**Kerry Konrady**, consumer-lifestyle brand-marketing executive

Are You Buying This?

What Americans Think about Money
and Life from an Advertising Propagandist

J. J. Robertson

Jupiter Books

Book Layout © 2016 Andrea Prieto

Cover design by *the*BookDesigners

Ordering Information:
Special discounts are available on quantity purchases by corporations, associations,
and others. For details, contact the "Special Sales Department" at the URL above.

Are You Buying This? What Americans Think about Money and Life from an Advertising
Propagandist/ J. J. Robertson. –1st ed.

For the people, by the people

"A dame that knows the ropes isn't likely to get tied up."

—Mae West

Contents

Acknowledgements

To Gillian Glover, Tracey Creech, Lori Ellison, Brooke Hodess,
everyone who answered my surveys, the team at Persuadable
Research, my family, my advertising family, the Viking,
the inventor of cake, and *you* for reading this. Enjoy.

Introduction

What do you think of Americans?

Do you believe they are smart, resilient, capable, and charming?

Or clueless, codependent, and celebrity obsessed?

Whatever you think—be prepared to change your mind. Because you're about to discover how thousands of women and men, aged 18 to 92, from Alaska to Wyoming, answered two of my nationwide surveys titled "Seize the Day" and "Show Me the Money," in which they revealed to me, a professional Brain Sucker®, the following:

- How they feel about their bosses and careers

- What they covet—from kinky boots to kinky men to condos

- What they think of themselves in the mirror

- What makes their "perfect day," and

- Where they get their wisdom

Also, as you find out more about Americans, you'll learn more about yourself, because the insight-packed chapters and fastidiously researched endnotes cover everything from behavioral economics and biological anthropology to psychology, sociology, and—wait for it—advertising. However, this is not an "advertising book." It will not teach you how to write copy that sells. Nor will it train you how to design compelling visuals that build brands. Lots of books do that already. Instead, you're about to discover what sort of information

I gather on consumers. Yes, my job is to understand "them"—which includes you. Because, full disclosure: I'm an advertising account planner. Consider yourself warned.

But before we dive enthusiastically into the chapters ahead, I want to clarify who this book is for, because our time together should be happy, productive, and mutually rewarding. Therefore:

- If you work in advertising or marketing, and you've yet to score a corner office—read on

- If you're an MBA student or a newbie entrepreneur—read on

- If you're a whip-smart undergraduate majoring in advertising, marketing, business, or mass communications—read on, or

- If you're fascinated by human nature and Americans, and you're hoping to read a succinct book of facts written by an expert who works in an industry where consumers get antsy mid-tweet—welcome

But if you're hoping to read a book packed with muscular buzzwords like "economic force-multiplier," or if you're hoping to read a tome packed with graphs and T-scores, this book is probably not for you (even though you're no doubt lovely). Go on, then . . . look away. I trust you'll find another book capable of bringing back memories of high-school statistics.

Still here? That's glorious. (Yes, I'm British.) You're going to learn a ton. Although, I'm concerned you might be stuck on the riddle of "What on earth is an account planner, anyhow?" So let's clear that up, before journeying together into the gray matter of American minds. Because I don't want you sitting there wondering whether account planners scour consumers' brains by dressing up like Spock from *Star Trek* and performing Vulcan mind-melds on the unsuspecting. When the truth is many of us hold graduate degrees in the social sciences. Even then, figuring out what makes people tick, and getting them to do our bidding, remains damnably hard. That's why I'm relieved most manufacturers go to extreme lengths to produce items they suspect you already want to buy (saving me the cost of buying pointy-eared prosthetics). Here's a definition of my job:

Account planners exist inside agencies to dig into and dissect the attitudes, aspirations, habits, and brand relationships of consumers. To acquire this data, we use a variety of qualitative and quantitative research techniques, from devising nationwide surveys with statistically significant results (like the surveys that form the basis to this book) to interviewing charming people inside their homes.

What happens to the data we collect? Well, the most useful bits we share with our teammates (e.g., art directors, copywriters, account managers, and media planners). Our mission? To ensure that everyone we work with has a sturdy foundation from which to create advertising concepts and campaigns that make consumers pause, then think, "I'm going to buy that now." Oh, and our data comes in handy during creative meetings, like whenever we're asked to give feedback on mocked-up ads through the eyes of the target audience. A role that has led to me saying stuff like, "As a 25-year-old man with two-day stubble and a girlfriend to get home to, I don't think I'd buy . . ." (Although, the less you know about that part of my job, the better.)

But what account planners don't do is, we don't normally share our work with a wider audience, because 1) information is power, whereby ad agencies protect their proprietary consumer data accordingly, and 2) our research is often subject to non-disclosure agreements, e.g., one of my clients was the U.S. Army, and nope, you're not getting their secrets today, so stop it with the puppy-dog eyes. But you are going to get an unprecedented peek into my world (*gulp*). However, to get the most out of it, which chapter should you read first?

Well, if you too are a researcher, start at Chapter Six. There, you'll discover how the study in this book was carried out. For example, (*deep inhale*) the Americans who answered my probing questions proportionately matched the latest U.S. census on:

- Ratio of men to women in America, and

- Ratio of residents in the Northeast to the South, West, and Midwest

While they closely matched the latest U.S. census on:

- Age distribution (although 30-plus-year-olds were slightly overrepresented)

- Ratio of Republican supporters to Democratic supporters

- Ratio of atheists to those with religious beliefs, and

- Ratio of U.S. citizens by birth to naturalized citizens

But if that list made you cross-eyed, start at Chapter One: there, the American people are waiting to meet you. They don't have all day. So, in the words of a Home Depot ad (that would have had an account planner like me working on it), "Let's do this."

Yours truly,

J. J. Robertson, the Brain Sucker

CHAPTER ONE

The Perfect Day

"If you want to make God laugh, tell him about your plans."

—Woody Allen

28,781. That's the average number of days each American gets to roam the earth until it's finger food at their funeral[1] About 10,000 of these days we spend asleep, leaving precious few for completing items on our bucket lists. Hence, the appeal of multi-tasking: "A mythical activity," says psychiatrist Edward Hallowell, "in which people believe they can perform two or more tasks simultaneously as effectively as one."[2] But if you were to imagine your perfect day, how would it begin? Where would you go? Who would be with you? And how would you feel? Would you want to be alert once more to the wonders around you, such as marveling at the colors of fall, or the flowers of spring? Or would you rather feel irresistible to your love interest, just as you are, with no need to spray yourself first in a scent named "Bratwursts & Beer" or "Fresh Minted Money"?

There are two reasons why I enjoy investigating the perfect day. One, the topic sheds light on the desires of consumers that helps my teammates devise campaigns that boost sales. Two, the topic sparks ideas for products my clients sometimes go on to manufacture, such as laptops with harder-to-break screens and video games in which the characters no longer resemble Justin Bieber (you're welcome). So what's the American "perfect day"?

Comfort, Joy, and "My Way"

When I asked folks to: *"Take a moment to visualize your perfect day. What leisure or work activities would you do?"* no two answers were quite the same due to everyone's different backgrounds, personality quirks, and the gazillion things we can get up to off- and online, from Elvis-impersonating in Reno to binge-watching on Netflix. But there were common themes, which you'd expect from folks with similar cultural values and DNA. Because, brace yourself for this: Your DNA sequence is about 99.9 percent identical to any person whom you care to mention, even though we often like to think of ourselves as being unique snowflakes.[3] But snowflakes are overrated, such a paltry lifespan, so what of the lifespan of the American perfect day? Here's a 24-hour timeline (that I compiled from thousands of responses to my surveys):

> **Morning.** On my perfect day, I'd awaken surrounded by warmth, softness, cleanliness, and comfort after about eight hours of sleep, having not been awakened by alarms, pets, humans, or the need to pee.[4] I'd be illness-, debt-, and pain-free (Woo-hoo!), as would the people I care about. If I had a bedmate, I'd love 'em, not loathe 'em. I'd have a movement on the porcelain throne.[5] And in the mirror, I'd be at peace with my saggy bits, or thrilled by my now-perky bits.

Then breakfast: I'd scarf the works, sip kale juice (and like it), or eat cake served to me. After which, if I went online, there'd be tales of goodwill, not of death or destruction. And as I dressed how I pleased, from cargo shorts to something sparkly that gets all eyes on me, I'd relax knowing I've no groceries to buy or objects to fix, giving me time for . . . (We'll get into people's specific activities shortly.)

Midday. Friends would join me for lunch, probably outdoors under a blue sky, with no risk of sunburn, bugs, or downpours soaking through underpants. Nearby would be water, from the ocean to a fountain. Our chitchat would be lively. Our relationships would feel closer. And after we'd eaten, I'd pay the bill happily, before heading off to (more activities), where, if I drove, the roads would be almost empty. If I flew, airlines once more would be generous with their complimentary nuts.

Evening. With my energy unflagging, I may try a new pastime prior to sunset before cooking dinner, or dining out with family and friends. The menu? Steak, lobster, burgers, or shrimp. The dessert, a classic. Drinks paired for the occasion. And as we ate, there'd be no jibes from belittling parents, or smart-arse remarks from kids, because today, "family fun" is not an oxymoron. After the meal, I'd gaze at the moon high in the sky above, while back in the bedroom, I would (activities).

Lights Out. Today was a success. No one was in crisis. No one had the flu. Public toilets were plentiful. (There were no lines of fidgeting women thinking: "Aha! That's what

Freud meant by penis envy.") And if I'd told someone, "I love you," they would've said it back to me with equal gusto. As I lie here in bed, ready for sleep, I've no nagging in my head and no worries for tomorrow.[6]

The American "perfect day" we've just read highlights our species' well-documented desire for *autonomy*, *personal growth*, and *a sense that our actions matter*. Throughout the timeline, most citizens acted like benevolent dictators, seeking control over their environments, their bodies, and their emotions, as well as the actions and well-being of others. The sun rose and set according to their preferences. Erections soared with no need for Viagra.[7] No one was broke. No adults or children bickered. No diapers dirtied. And, the world was a haven of decency. (Cue beauty-pageant organizers cheering, "We did it, ladies! We got world peace.")

In addition, on their perfect day, many individuals reported feeling renewed, partly because they'd imagined themselves experimenting with their five senses, e.g., in terms of vision, going outdoors can lower our blood pressure (as can watching nature videos). And, on the perfect day, many folks saw themselves on beaches and mountaintops scanning the horizon as far as their eyes could see.[8] Also in terms of taste, smell, and mouth-feel, one of the most-cited meals was steak (an umami-rich food) that, when eaten, increases our brain's production of norepinephrine and dopamine: two neurochemicals that, in the words of biological anthropologist Helen Fisher, "play a crucial role in sexual arousal."[9] (Making Buenos Aires—a city famed for T-Bones and tango—a sultry destination.)

But while the American perfect day might sound pretty back-to-basics, in that it features relatively simple pleasures, and had

I asked the question 50 years ago, I might have received similar responses. It's worth stating that people's descriptions were also rife with mentions of and allusions to modern luxuries that bring us comfort and joy, such as air-conditioning, high-thread count sheets, ergonomic mattresses, dishwashers, triple-glazed windows, smooth-riding cars, and power showers. That's why movements like "simple living" have yet to sweep the nation, as most folks like their comforts. (Cue corporations doing fist-pumps.)

What Do You Like to Do?

When I was 13 years of age, my feet outgrew the ladies' footwear departments in almost every store in my hometown of Edinburgh, Scotland. Consequently, as I was now a size 10 U.S., my choice in footwear became restricted to men's sneakers, men's lace-up oxfords (that were fitted alongside my father's), and red-patent stilettos (that—if my mother had let me wear them—would've been fitted alongside the latex-curious in the local fetish store). But even if my feet had been dainty, I'd probably still prefer hiking to browsing Jimmy Choos, because the stuff we like to do is influenced by our biology, our psychology, and our environment—a group of factors I affectionately call "the big three."

In regard to psychology, you're about to find out how, in my study, a person's self-assessment of their dominant personality type influenced which activities they wanted to do on their perfect day. First, here's a cheat sheet to the types (don't worry, there won't be an exam):

In 1979, social psychologist Thomas Bouchard began researching twins who had been parted at birth and raised apart to examine to what extent their temperaments and hobbies were similar. His trailblazing work, which asked the question: "How much of our personality is due to nature versus nurture?" led to the famous *Minnesota Twin Family Study* (a longitudinal dataset that quantifies genetic-heritability estimates of behavior syndromes and traits, arising from complexes of genes working together—go team!). The accuracy of the dataset is contentious, but when psychologists David Lykken and Auke Tellegen trawled through it, they calculated that for traits like anger, anxiety, and curiosity, heritability appears to play about 50 percent of the role in temperamental variations. For subjective well-being, it plays about 80 percent of the role. In plain English, whether or not you're a twin, if your parents are bubbly, chances are, you are too.[10]

Furthermore, because the nature-nurture debate has fascinated so many researchers, a slew of evidence exists to suggest there are four broad personality types. Each of us is a mixture of all four, with one of the types typically dominant. Over two thousand years ago, the Greek philosopher Plato named these types the Rational, Guardian, Artisan, and Idealist.[11] But we're going to use the names Helen Fisher gave to the types in her recent book, *Why Him, Why Her?*, as I'm fed up with the term *artisan*, because the word *artisanal* has been overused in ads. Here are her summaries:

Director (Rational)

"Directors can tolerate extreme isolation, long hours at the desk and many other discomforts when they work. But they must pursue their goals and solve their problems on their own. . . . Many strive for one of life's highest prizes: knowledge."

Builder (Guardian)

"Builders pride themselves in being orderly . . . they don't like unpredictability. . . . [They] feel comfortable in hierarchies—where duty and loyalty are required, and structure, rules, and order reign."

Explorer (Artisan)

"Explorers seek adventures of the mind and senses. They are intensely curious and unusually creative. They are restless, energetic and spontaneous. . . . They are willing to risk a great deal to pursue their many interests."[12]

Negotiator (Idealist)

"Negotiators [have an] exquisite awareness of everything around them. . . . They adopt causes and choose careers to improve human welfare. . . . For them, self-discovery is a quest."[13]

So what did these personality types want to do differently on their perfect day?

Well, Directors typically wanted to start their day by browsing news headlines and emails, before watching tightly plotted movies, solving work challenges, dining at best-of-the-best restaurants, drinking fine wines, visiting museums, or thrashing their opponents at sports with scoring systems, because directors enjoy quantifying their wins.[14]

Builders typically stayed inside or close to their homes in leafy suburbs. Where their favorite activities included antiquing, baking, admiring fall foliage, coaching little league, playing video games, and, most importantly, sitting around tables with their nearest and dearest for home-cooked meals, free of melodrama.[15]

Explorers often talked of collecting heart-racing thrills, such as going skiing, whooping on roller coasters, rocketing to the moon, quad-biking across deserts, kayaking along lost rivers, eating spicy foods, and dancing barefoot on beaches to live music under warm starry skies.[16]

And, out of the four types, Negotiators' descriptions most often featured the words *relax*, *quiet*, and *guilt-free*. As well as the word long, as in long baths, long back rubs, long movie nights, long walks . . .[17] Because unlike Explorers, Negotiators more often wanted to pursue Zen-like activities on their perfect day—albeit some fancied revving up their "Om shanti" bliss with heart-quickening moments like kissing in candlelit rooms. From their lips to your reading material:

> *"I would spend the day with the woman I had wanted to marry, but she married another. I wouldn't care where we were, or what we did. I just want to spend it with her."*
> —Negotiator from Nebraska, aged 49, never married

And:

> *"I would wake with the one I love, make love, shower, eat breakfast, and hike with my family. Then I would come home, have a wonderful dinner, make love, and sleep in the arms of my one-and-only."*
> —Negotiator from Illinois, aged 36, on her second marriage

One reason why Negotiators often fancied curling up with someone on their perfect day is that hugs are their drug of choice; cuddling releases the hormone oxytocin (a mood regulator) that can lessen anxiety, which Negotiators often suffer from chronically due to the amount of energy they invest in catering to the needs of others.[18] But (spoiler alert!) in the following table, you'll notice every type wanted to love and be loved on their perfect day, as one of *the* most-cited pastimes across all types was "being with family." But what about, err, you know, sex?

Most-Mentioned Activities/Desires on the Perfect Day by Dominant Personality Type

	DIRECTOR		BUILDER		EXPLORER		NEGOTIATOR
1	Being with family	1	Being with family	1	Going outdoors	1	Being with family
2	Going outdoors	2	Eating dinner	2	Being with family	2	Going outdoors
3	Watching TV or movies	3	Being at home	3	Relaxing	3	Being at home
4=	Going to the beach	4	Being with children	4	Going to the beach	4	Watching TV or movies
4=	Eating dinner	5	Playing video games	5	Exercising solo, e.g., running	5	Being with children
4=	Playing sports	6	Going outdoors	6	Going for a walk	6	Being with friends
7	Reading news/ nonfiction	7	Walking the neighborhood	7	Being with friends	7	Going for a walk
8	Relaxing	8	Watching TV or movies	8	Being in the sun	8	Going to the beach
9	Being with friends	9	Enjoying breakfast	9	Playing in or on the ocean	9	Eating dinner
10	Feeling successful	10	Going to the beach	10	Playing team sports	10	Feeling like I have no worries

Who's in the Mood?

Advertisers use sexual imagery in ads to sell almost anything. For example, in the U.K., an infamous commercial for Cadbury's Flake in the 1980s showed a woman essentially giving a blowjob to the aforementioned six-inch chocolate bar, which, when I was a teen, made me reticent to unwrap them in public, out of concern that I might over-excite passersby. While today in the U.S., hair-flicking, husky-voiced women smolder in ads selling cat food to sneakers. But considering the amount of sexual innuendo in ads, you might be surprised by how few Americans admitted to wanting "nudge, nudge, wink, wink" on their perfect day.

In the preceding table, sex was notably absent. That's because among Explorers, sex was their 12th most-mentioned activity; among Directors, their 16th; Builders, their 17th, and Negotiators, their 27th. In terms of percentages, this works out to fewer than 10 percent of Explorers, Directors, and Builders; and fewer than five percent of Negotiators talked of naked shenanigans. (Their fantasies varying from getting steamy between the sheets with their spouse for longer than three minutes to red-hot flings where nipples would be expertly attended to, rather than ham-fistedly twiddled like dials on a cooker: a little to the right, she might turn on.)[19]

However, statistics on carnal desire are as unreliable as the pull-out method. Perversely, that's no tragedy even for a serious researcher like me. Because if exact data on sexual desire existed, folks giving answers on the far sides of a distribution curve could feel further pressured by society to conform and perform accordingly. At present, there is no "normal." It's a good thing. Besides, more

Negotiators might've included sex on their perfect day were it not for their 10th most-cited activity/desire: to have no worries. If you're in love with a Negotiator, this quote is for you:

> *"On my perfect day, my meals would be prepared by a chef. My husband and I would see a great movie. We would have fun discussing it over a meal. We would make passionate love, and end up exhausted on freshly washed sheets smelling of lavender."*
> —61-year-old Negotiator from Texas, on her second marriage

That's right, for Negotiators, obliterating their laundry duties and other chores arguably rivals oysters as an aphrodisiac, because the fewer errands they have, the more amorous some of them become.

And Who Wanted to Shop?

The U.S. sells every temptation, from caramel cupcakes to video-camera drones that buzz the air over your neighbors' backyards. (Binoculars and curtain twitching are so '50s Hitchcock.) But when Americans described their perfect day, only three percent mentioned shopping. And those who did spoke mostly of snapping up souvenirs (to serve as mementoes to this fine glorious day), rather than discounted saucepans and other items punched over in Black Friday brawls. What's intriguing about this snub of retail is even citizens with compulsive buying disorders—of which an estimated six percent of the U.S. population will experience at some point in their lives—seldom spoke of shopping on their perfect day.[20] That's why retailers typically schedule their deepest discounts and splashiest ad campaigns around major holidays, because if they failed to slash and advertise their slashed prices, it's likely more of their customers would be outdoors, not in stores, or at home with family and friends, as opposed to at home, online shopping.[21]

Now a question for you:

What is your bartering arrangement for *your* perfect day?

- Would you ditch your plans in favor of shopping, if your favorite stores were to give you 10 percent off all your purchases? How about 50 percent off?

- Or, if you're holding steady, how much of a discount would it take for you to spend some of your perfect day purchasing my clients' goods?[22] (The smaller the discount you ask for, the more my clients will adore you.)

Brain Fuel: If You Study/Work in Advertising

What would happen on your perfect day?

What would happen on your worst day?

Name two brands that appeal to the Director personality type.

Name two brands that appeal to the Builder personality type.

Name two brands that appeal to the Explorer personality type.

Name two brands that appeal to the Negotiator personality type.

Name three brands that encourage consumers to experiment with all five senses.

Name three brands that offer enjoyable online shopping experiences to consumers.

Brain Fuel: If You Study/Work in Marketing

What would happen on your perfect day?

What would happen on your worst day?

Name three products/services that help the Director personality type to enjoy their perfect day.

Name three products/services that help the Builder personality type to enjoy their perfect day.

Name three products/services that help the Explorer personality type to enjoy their perfect day.

Name three products/services that help the Negotiator personality type to enjoy their perfect day.

Think of one of your favorite products. How would you improve its sensory characteristics to give folks with your dominant personality type greater pleasure?

Fieldwork for All

Spend a day visiting the highest and lowest landmarks in your neighborhood. As you gaze out from these different landmarks, think about how it makes you feel.

Organize a potluck with your friends where the dishes run the gamut from sour to sweet.

Visit a garden center to discover your favorite scent.

Go to Noisli.com and discover which background noises boost your productivity and which relax you.

Spend a day touching items (so long as it doesn't get you into trouble), from running your fingers through faux sheepskin Ikea rugs to walking barefoot on sand.

Notes

1. Average life expectancy in the U.S. is 78.8 years. But not every year we're alive feels the same duration. That's because as we age, routine typically infiltrates our days, creating fewer memories for us to look back on, making recent years feel briefer and faster than expected. (Claudia Hammond, *Time Warped: Unlock the Mysteries of Time Perception*; CDC, 2013 data.)

2. Edward Hallowell's quote is from *Crazy Busy: Overstretched, Overbooked and About to Snap!*

3. Former President Bill Clinton once said, "The most important fact of life is our common humanity." If the term "common humanity" gives you the heebie-jeebies, find out why in Marilynn B. Brewer, "The Social Self: On Being the Same and Different at the Same Time," *Personality and Social Psychology Bulletin*, 1991; 17:475–82.

4. *Nocturia* (the need to get up to pee in the night) is a major cause of sleep loss in the U.S. In a 2003 National Sleep Foundation poll, 65 percent of 55- to 84-year-olds in their sample were affected by *nocturia* several nights per week (sleepfoundation.org).

5. Constipation affects roughly 15 percent of the U.S. population. (Peter D. R. Higgins and John F. Johanson, "Epidemiology of Constipation in North America: A Systematic Review," *American Journal of Gastroenterology*, 2004; 99:750–759.)

6. The three most commonly used verbs in people's descriptions of their perfect day were *go, enjoy*, and *eat*. Global brands like Coca-Cola and Visa have used these words with tactical precision in their taglines.

7. Manufacturers use vanity sizing on clothing to boost the self-esteem of their consumers, e.g., medium-sized garments are often labeled as "small"—the reverse is true for condoms and bras. A marketing director for a condom manufacturer told me, "We'd go bankrupt selling condoms in small, medium, and large." Hence, the popular selling "XL-size." I'm waiting on the OMG-size. (JoAndrea Hoegg and others, "The Flip Side of Vanity Sizing: How Consumers Respond to and Compensate for Larger than Expected Clothing Sizes," *Journal of Consumer Psychology*, 2014; 24(1):70–78.)

8. As Helen Fisher explains, "[As] primates we gather over 80 percent of our knowledge of the world around us with our eyes." We love to look. What's more, according to Richard Dawkins, "[Our] high-quality color vision with [its] three-color system may have evolved in our primate ancestors as an aid to finding fruits in the green forest." (Helen Fisher, *Why We Love: The Nature and Chemistry of Romantic Love*; Richard Dawkins, *Unweaving the Rainbow: Science, Delusion, and the Appetite for Wonder*, and Roger Ulrich and others, "Stress Recovery during Exposure to Natural and Urban Environments," *Journal of Environmental Psychology*, 1991; 11(3):201–230.)

9. Dining on lobster or steak does more than stimulate the production of neurochemicals inside our bodies; when people order costly entrées in public, it signifies to others that the orderer might be high in status. For more, read Carlin Flora, "The Protein-Hunger Connection," in *Psychology Today*. Jan. 23, 2006; Helen Fisher, *Why We Love: The Nature and Chemistry of Romantic Love*.

10. For more on the *Minnesota Twin Family Study*, read Thomas J. Bouchard Jr. and others, "Sources of Human Psychological Differences: The Minnesota Study of Twins Reared Apart," *Science*, 1990; 4978:223–228.

11. Plato's student Aristotle believed that people strive for happiness in one of four ways: logical investigation, acquiring assets, sensuous pleasure, or moral virtue. These ways relate to Plato's personality types: Rational, Guardian, Artisan, and Idealist. However, a woman who pursues logical investigation is not necessarily disinterested in decorating her home, bodice-ripping sex, or helping others; she's just more often focused on the need-to-know. Tangent: In the 1970s, psychologist David Keirsey incorporated Plato's types into his well-known psychological questionnaire, the "Keirsey Temperament Sorter." For more, check out David Keirsey and Marilyn Bates, *Please Understand Me II: Temperament, Character, Intelligence.*

12. According to Helen Fisher, an Explorer's lust for life is partly due to "elevated activity in the mesolimbic dopamine system . . . high circulating testosterone; low serotonin in many limbic regions; and low norepinephrine in [their] cerebrospinal fluid." (Helen Fisher, *Why Him? Why Her?*)

13. If you're wondering how respondents in my study assessed their dominant personality type, I asked them the following: *"Which of these four descriptions is most like your personality: 1 = Most like me, 2 = Second closest, 3 = Third closest, 4 = Least like me*
    - *You are highly energetic, crave novelty and adventure, and love to travel;*
    - *You manage people (from employees to family) effectively, value traditions, are highly organized, and prefer predictability to unpredictability;*
    - *You are focused, logical, and competitive; enjoy intellectual debates; and make decisions with ease; Or,*
    - *You are empathic, emotionally expressive, trust your intuition, and have deep friendships."*

14. Directors don't want everything under the sun; when there is something they want, they tend to want the best. Mercedes' tagline, "The best or nothing," speaks directly to this type, as do many ads citing statistics, as Directors enjoy quantifying the excellence of their purchases to themselves and others.

15. Builders who saw themselves vacationing on their perfect day often chose locations offering many of the comforts of home like Disney World, the Hawaiian Islands, or cruise ships. Explorers more often thought: "Thailand. Tequila. Teeny bikini."

16. In psychology labs, when human subjects listen to cheerful music, their moods typically elevate for 10 to 15 minutes. Music is a temporary mood modulator as are alcohol, caffeine, cocaine, chocolate, gambling, nicotine, opiates, and shopping. Over reliance on such modulators can lead to addictive patterns. (Michael Argyle, *The Psychology of Happiness*.)

17. Language is imprecise, e.g., Negotiators in my study typically used the word "marathon" as a synonym for "long" (e.g., marathon movie nights), whereas Explorers used it to describe long-distance running races. That's why ad agencies copy-test ads to ensure the target audience gets something close to the client's intended message.

18. For more on oxytocin, read Heon-Jin Lee and others, "Oxytocin: The Great Facilitator of Life," *Progress in Neurobiology*, 2009; 88(2):127–151.

19. The eldest respondent to mention sex on their perfect day was a 76-year-old divorcée from Texas.

20. To understand more about shopping addiction, read Donald W. Black, "A Review of Compulsive Buying Disorder," *World Psychiatry*, 2007; 6(1):14–18.

21. Over 90 years ago, department-store owner John Wanamaker apparently said, "I know half the money I spend on advertising is wasted, but I can never find out which half." But Mr. Wanamaker kept hiring copywriters, because without their artful sales techniques, he suspected his Philadelphian customers might do other things with their time and money than visit his store, especially on national holidays.

22. This chapter discussed the American perfect day for the majority of my respondents. But roughly 10 percent of my respondents described alternate perfect days. Common events on these days included: witnessing the resurrection of a loved one, getting away with murder, and awakening cured from a pre-existing terminal illness. However, similar to the majority of my respondents, they seldom mentioned shopping. This may be because many of these people were depressed: and when we're depressed, as opposed to deeply unhappy, we're less inclined to shop.

CHAPTER TWO

Money

*"Never confuse the size of your
paycheck with the size of your talent."*
—Marlon Brando

If I were a money-grubbing account planner, I'd have written, instead of this book, *How to Be a Millionaire While Barely Trying: Shortcuts to the Destiny You Were Born to Fulfill.* My pen name would ooze gravitas—perhaps I'd be Ulysses Black. And my target audience would be wannabe corporate titans eager for wealth.

"Dear Reader," it would begin, "This book is about having it all. You name it, it's yours: gold-plated toilets, Gulfstream jets . . . Read on, I'll explain." After which, I would re-flog the law of attraction (a.k.a., "if you can dream it, you can do it"), while I peppered in data on magnetic currents, quotes from Napoleon Hill's *Think and Grow Rich*, and tips on how to build a personal brand while seated in a La-Z-Boy chair.

But unlike my greedy alter ego (whom I imagine is on a yacht in Saint-Tropez, burning paper currency to light her cigars) I'd feel guilty that my readers would soon awaken from their warm suspensions of belief into a world where success is seldom easy. And while you might expect someone who helps make ads that exaggerate the truth (a lot) to enjoy shoveling platitudes for profit, truth be told, many people in advertising aren't keen on it. I am (sometimes) one of them.

That's why this chapter won't instruct you on how to get rich-through-idleness; my conscience won't allow it (humph), and such a chapter would be one sentence long: "Write down the amount of loot you want, wish for it, ta-dah!"

Instead, it explores the more valuable question: How does money fit into the American Dream? The answer is important to know, because 1) it might cause you to reassess your views on money, and 2) one of the oldest tricks in the ad-land book is to hint to customers, if they buy "X," they'll get one step closer to contentment. But to use (or resist) this tactic, you must know what people desire.

I Spy . . .

When I asked folks, *"During the last six months, have you noticed an item in somebody's possession you would like to own?"*

- 49 percent of Americans said, "Oh, yes!"

- 40 percent said, "I've not seen anything I fancy"

- 11 percent said, "I have everything I want"

Don't put too much stock in these percentages; had the question been asked on December 24, more Americans would likely have said,

"Oh, yes!" to coveting! That's why we're going to focus on people's objects of desire, rather than dwelling on those statistics. And (spoiler alert!) as homes were one of the most drooled over objects in the U.S. (I hear you; Realtor.com is my porn), I've separated out what homeowners had been lusting after versus non-homeowners. (Dramatic pause.)

Homeowners who'd been coveting others' goods most often admitted to ogling that person's (in reverse order of popularity): lover, big toys (e.g., jet skis), disposable income, clothing/accessories, home, gadgets. In first place? Their vehicle. While coveting non-homeowners appeared to share similar desires, except in the realm of big toys—powerboats and the like are seldom a priority when you rent[2] But between and within these groups lurked major differences. Can you spot them?

Non-homeowners

> *"Due to the economy and my finances, I have denied myself a lot. A decent automobile and new shoes would make me happy right now."*
> —40-year-old divorcée from Ohio who dislikes her career

> *"I want a pair of stylish sunglasses instead of my prescription ones."*
> —29-year-old who wants to date, and has two jobs

> *"My dream is as simple as having a place of my own and being able to decorate it as I please."*
> —Married thirty-something in Silicon Valley

Mortgage-holders

"My house is full of stuff. I want a larger tidy home with nicer furniture."

—Divorced grandma who admits to fantasies
where a hit-man guns down her ex

"I want a new Jeep Wrangler and my high school sweetheart."

—Self-employed Floridian, age 29,
who married someone else

Homeowners without mortgages

"I want a home with an inside swimming pool, six bedrooms, five baths, a games room, decked-out kitchen, and a high-priced vehicle."

—35-year-old, solo-living lawyer who said
she wants her ex to envy her

And:

"A Rolex."

—New Yorker, age 53, whose passion is fashion

Together these quotes reveal three familiar trends:

- Our propensity to covet surges when we are unhappy at home or at work[3]

- A person can like designer treats without demanding non-stop bling, e.g., toilet plungers encrusted in Swarovski crystals and Evian bathwater, and

- Non-homeowners who'd been coveting goods most often wanted items that get labeled as basic to mid-range; whereas, homeowners (especially those without mortgages) most often wanted luxury versions of stuff they already owned . . .[4]

The sweaters they'd been pining for were cashmere, not cotton.[5] The phones they'd been after were this season's, not last. And the scents gents fancied self-spritzing were more likely to be *Acqua di Giò* than Axe Africa (a mass-produced body deodorant with the subtlety of formaldehyde).

But pungent odors aside, the question is: "When we get what we covet, does our subjective well-being increase?"

Yes, yes it does. Unless we are:

- Already at the top of our happiness range

- Undergoing emotional/physical turmoil that can smother joy, or

- Getting something that 1) upsets our loved ones, 2) requires constant maintenance, or 3) is suited to someone else's biology, personality, or environment, e.g., we relocate to the wilderness when our heart belongs to the city, or we buy clothes too small for us when we should've bought ones that fit

But as you know, happiness boosts associated with the acquisition of goods are typically fleeting—with the exception of big-ticket items that rise us into the middle-class like cars with exhausts that don't scrape along roads, or thick-walled condos that blanket the neighbors' squabbles. But (psst!) there are ways to prolong your shopper's high. Two are:

- Buy items suited to your pleasures (for me, that includes hiking boots for wooded adventures and tea strainers that minister to my addiction to Earl Grey), or

- Get rare or unique items, like handmade furniture, that hamper the ability of frenemies to make snarky one-upmanship comments, such as "Mine's bigger, stronger, faster" (I know yours is, Veronica. There's no need to brag.)[6]

But let me ask you this: "Whom do we covet from the most?" In the Bible, it was the Joneses. "You shall not covet your neighbor's house," Exodus 20:17 (NIV) declares, "[And] you shall not covet your neighbor's wife, or his male or female servant, his ox or ass, or anything that belongs to your neighbor." (This from an era when an ox was as enviable as a Mercedes. And the word "ass" referred to the animal, not a noteworthy booty.)

But today, the Joneses' possessions are not Americans' most wanted. Among my respondents, women who'd been coveting goods, most often said the items had belonged to their friends (but not their best friends, with whom their relationships are less calculative), followed by items owned by unacquainted women, unacquainted men, neighbors, and, in equal fifth place, sisters or coworkers.[7]

While men who'd been coveting goods most often said items belonged to unacquainted men, friends (again, not their best dudes), neighbors, and, in equal fourth place, brothers, coworkers, or unacquainted women. So, if you answered, "Whom do we covet from the most?" with "Friends (not BFFs) who are often similar in status and in age to us, followed by strangers who are often the same gender as us," you get a gold star.[8]

Sidebar: Vehicles

A few years ago, an auto executive for a manufacturer with plunging sales told me, "Women don't like cars." Ridiculous, narrow-minded auto exec! More women in my study said they'd been lusting after vehicles than Tom Cruise, hairdos, or other things ladies supposedly bleat on about *ad nauseam*. Many women adore flooring 200-mph dream machines—their cars obeying their mistresses' bidding— while others have been known to gaze at vehicles offering greater fuel economy, trunk capacity, and reliability than their present rides. Their desires related to factors like the length of their gas-guzzling commutes, 2-for-1 supermarket promos on bulky items like toilet paper, and their concerns over personal safety. Because women (and men) know that in the U.S. there are areas where breakdowns can prove fatal. (*Frozen* is no Disney musical, if your engine conks out in Alaska.)

But I'll give this to that auto executive: in my study, home-owning men who'd been coveting cars most often wanted either:

- Iconic expensive cars from their adolescence like vintage Rolls-Royces (if they'd been teens in the '60s), or classic Ferraris (if they'd been teens in the '80s), or [9]

- Top-of-the-range new German cars (which is bad news for the U.S. auto industry)[10]

Whereas home-owning car-leering women seemed more open to a wider variety of brands and price points than did the men, with more of them naming Japanese and American cars. That's good news for Detroit and, incidentally, good news for the auto exec who worked for a Japanese company!

So, What Do People Desire?

Americans want their American Dream. No two versions of it are quite the same, but the basic tenets resemble historian Jared Diamond's definition of a first-world lifestyle: "acquiring a house, appliances, utensils, clothes, and consumer products . . . having access to manufactured modern medicines, and to doctors and dentists . . . eating abundant food . . . traveling by motor vehicle transport . . . and having access to other products manufactured elsewhere."[11] To which I'll add: giving and receiving love, being able to aid family and friends, living life with a sense of purpose, and watching acronym-named TV-shows like *NCIS*. (Never underestimate the appeal of silver fox Mark Harmon.) Once we have these things, we covet less. (Of the 11 percent of folks in my study who said, "I have everything I want," most had every item on that list.)

But as you know, getting the American Dream can be tricky for non-Mayflower descendants.[12] Eighteen percent of my respondents said, "I don't have an American Dream," with men (in general) more dispirited than women. (That's likely related to men often having higher initial expectations of success than women; blokes aren't supposed to hit glass ceilings and the like.) Plus, West Coast residents (in general) were more disheartened than folks elsewhere. The region's figure was skewed by California, where 25 percent of my respondents said they don't have an American Dream.[13] Their disappointment likely tied to practical considerations, such as California's steep real-estate prices, as well as higher expectations of success fueled by the California Dream: that's like the American Dream, but with more sun, and the allure of quicker fortunes for the bold—a throwback to the state's Gold Rush era.[14] No wonder, many Californians have considered relocating to where their American Dream might be somewhat affordable. Others have slashed their goals:

> *"[All I want is] to pay off my student loans before I die."*
> —23-year-old who wants a job in finance to get out of debt

> *"I've been unemployed since my job was outsourced to India. I'd worked there 31 years. My dream is to provide for my family in a modest fashion."*
> —51-year-old mortgagee with over $10,000 in credit card debt[15]

Yet when I asked folks across the country, *"How much extra money per year (tax-free) would it take for you to feel more content?"* how much do you think each person asked for?[16] A million? A billion? Or perhaps Einstein was on the money when he said, "Too many of us look upon Americans as dollar chasers. This is a cruel libel, even if it is reiterated thoughtlessly by the Americans themselves."

Who Wants to Be a Billionaire

There's nothing romantic about living in hovels with drafts, roaches, and mold the color of pond slime. The best things in life are often free. But poverty is fearsome; money is marvelous. With it, rotten teeth can get transformed into pearly whites; dining out can occur not only via vending machines. Also, cash lets us indulge in our passions—

from collecting outfits for pets to exploring castles under windswept skies. (For which, sidebar, I recommend visiting Scotland, where the greatest mystery isn't "Does the Loch Ness Monster exist?" It's, "Does that man have ~~a monster~~ underpants on beneath his kilt?")

But as you know from being a denizen of the modern world, having big bucks is no guarantor of happiness. Because as my respondents were swift to point out:

- Money can buy you sex, but it can't buy you love— among my married respondents, the very rich and the very poor were most worried their spouses were about to divorce them for someone wealthier[17]

- The superrich get targeted by the paparazzi (I, for one, would rather live with less than have my beach body splattered across the *National Enquirer*), and

- Cash windfalls, like winning the lottery, can upend the scaffolding of people's lives, toppling friendships

With this in mind, here are some highlights on how much extra tax-free money, Americans asked for (per year):

- People earning the full-time minimum-wage often sought an extra $35,000 per annum, rocketing their personal incomes into the ballpark of the U.S. median household income of around $52,000[18]

- Those on higher salaries often wanted an extra $50,000 per annum, zooming many of their personal incomes into six-figures

- Men (on average) requested $8,500 more than the amounts asked for by most women

- Folks in the West (on average) asked for $7,000 more than the amounts asked for by folks elsewhere

- 7 percent of the nation requested $0 (many of whom were in the "I have everything I want" group), and

- 22 percent of the nation requested an extra $1 million or more per annum[19]

In summary, the poor and lower-middle class generally seemed focused on attaining the monetary lifestyles of the middle class, the middle class on the upper-middle class, and upwards of that? Fewer Americans than you might've expected asked for sums that would've made them billionaires, a group whose hardships include being dumped by their lingerie-model girlfriends for Leonardo DiCaprio.

But are these statistics remotely accurate, considering almost half of American adults play the lottery in any given year? (Albeit many only play during rollovers to get in on water-cooler conversations at work.)[20]

Some folks probably did downplay their desires, as many religious groups and many more counter-culture movements frown on blatant excess, and those answering my questions had no idea who'd be reading their comments. But another likely explanation for the sums asked for is, when I asked Americans, *"What's the best way to get money: borrow it, earn it, inherit it, marry it, or win it?"* 74 percent said, "Earn it."[21]

And there's no reason to suspect all 74 percent are lying; psychologically, our species is hardwired to seek out and enjoy rewards from our labors.[22] Also, in the U.S., self-made men and women command far more respect than jackpot winners or trust-funders.[23] We like to feel respected. Therefore, as my respondents mulled over how much extra cash it would take to make them more content, it's likely many of them chose sums that (at a push) they thought they could earn in the near future—allowing them to earn their American Dream.[24] Yet, it's also likely many of them have dreamt of living it large, if only for one day, just to see what it's like. I know, I have. (In fact, I'm dreaming of it right now as you finish this sentence.)

Brain Fuel: If You Study/Work in Advertising

Think of a brand. Name five items this brand's target audience can't live without.

Thinking of the same brand, how have the tastes of its target audience evolved in the past five years, e.g., their tastes in music, food, and fashion?

Watch six commercials on the "advertcar" channel on YouTube. As you watch each commercial think about its target audience. Take into consideration their age-range, sex, and dominant personality type (Director, Builder, Explorer, or Negotiator).

When the movies *Transformers 1*, *2* and *3* came out, Chevrolet Camaro sales rose to #1 in their vehicle's category, in part thanks to the heroism of Bumblebee the Camaro-transforming Autobot (media. chevrolet.com). Name two other car manufacturers that have used product-placement effectively in movies.

Brain Fuel: If You Study/Work in Marketing

Think of a product category, e.g., vodka or men's clothing. In this category, which brand do you believe the target audience covets the most, and which do they covet the least? Next, research sales figures for this category, paying attention to which brand, last year, generated the biggest profits.

When designing products, it pays to consider whether your target audience rent or have mortgages, e.g., removable wall decals are great for renters: clunky furniture is not. Name three recent product launches that appealed most to renters, and three that appealed most to mortgage holders.

Shortly after I bought my Volkswagen GTI, the dealership mailed me a package containing a "VW Fast" toy. (Confused? Type "VW Fast" into Amazon's search field.) This post-sales tactic extended my shoppers' high, while giving me another reason to bore my friends about my car. Name two other post-sales tactics that car companies have used to extend the shoppers' high of their drivers.

Fieldwork for All

Identify three items in your home that give you as much pleasure now (or almost as much pleasure now) as when you got them. Are these items rare or unique? And/or, do these items help you to enjoy your greatest pleasures?

Ask a friend to describe her or his American Dream. Now ask them how their dream has changed.

Spend an evening watching movies you loved as a teen. Pay attention to the vehicles. Do you still have a crush on any of them? (Thanks to *Back to the Future*, I ♥ cars with gull-wing doors.)

Identify three items in your home you seldom used after buying them. Try to recall what had been going on in your psychology, biology, and your environment at the time of purchase, e.g., Had the items been on sale? Had you recently been in an argument? Or, perhaps it had been raining for weeks and you'd thought, "Stuff this. I need a treat"?

Notes

1. Our propensity to covet is influenced by our biology, psychology, and our environment, e.g., alcohol, hunger, sale signs, and fatigue affect our ability to control our emotions and our behavior, making us grab what we otherwise wouldn't. As Steven Pinker writes: "Alcohol interferes with synaptic transmission throughout the cerebrum, especially in the prefrontal cortex, the region responsible for self-control. An inebriated brain is less inhibited sexually, verbally, and physically." (Steven Pinker, *The Better Angels of Our Nature*.)

2. In my study, 41 percent of homeowners and 59 percent of non-homeowners admitted to coveting others' goods during the last six months. Among homeowners, 38 percent said they had been eyeing other people's vehicles; 24 percent, their gadgets; 21 percent, their homes; 5 percent, their clothing and accessories; 5 percent, their disposable income (a.k.a., money); 4.5 percent, their big toys, and about 1 percent, their relationships. Among non-homeowners: 36 percent admitted to ogling other people's vehicles; 24 percent, their gadgets; 23 percent, their homes; 6 percent, their clothes and accessories; 4 percent, their money, and 4 percent, their relationships.

3. We more often covet others' goods when we're fed up with cupid. In my study, 65 percent of single women who'd said they want to date admitted to coveting others' goods in the last six months; whereas among single women who said they're happy being solo, only 44 percent said they'd been coveting others' goods.

4. For more on the hedonic treadmill, read Daniel Kahneman, Edward Diener, and Norbert Schwarz (eds.) *Well-Being: Foundations of Hedonic Psychology*.

5. Mark Twain said, "Clothes make the man. Naked people have little or no influence on society." It's not whimsical to want to be smart-dressed.

6. "Economists and psychologists have spent decades studying the relation between wealth and happiness," psychologist Daniel Gilbert explains, "And they have generally concluded that wealth increases human happiness when it lifts people out of abject poverty and into the middle class but that it does little to increase happiness thereafter." Yet as economist Robert Frank states, "It is a serious misreading of the evidence . . . to conclude that absolute living standards do not matter. What the data seem to say is that as national income grows, people do not spend their extra money in ways that yield significant and lasting increases in measured satisfaction." (Daniel Gilbert, *Stumbling on Happiness*; Robert Frank, *Luxury Fever*.)

7. As Alain de Botton wrote in reference to Greek philosopher Epicurus's teachings: "True friends do not evaluate us according to world criteria . . . like ideal parents, their love for us remains unaffected by our appearance or position in the social hierarchy . . ." (Alain de Botton, *The Consolations of Philosophy*.)

8. In my study, only three percent of "coveters" said they'd been eyeing goods belonging to celebrities. Among these three percent, many lived in California and/or said they were interested in careers that bring fame. Tangent: We typically covet goods belonging to people who are similar in age to us. There are exceptions. Many grandparents in my study said they'd been coveting their grandkids' gadgets.

9. The 1980s TV series *Magnum P.I.* and the 1986 movie *Ferris Bueller's Day Off* both starred Ferraris. No surprise, many American men who'd been boys in '80s lusted after Italians other than Sophia Loren.

10. If German luxury-car brands weren't so prestigious among American luxury-car buyers, non-German companies like Jaguar, Lincoln, and Infiniti might be able to lower their marketing budgets. As it stands, in 2013, Jaguar spent $4,000 on measured media per car that it sold in the U.S; Lincoln spent $2,728 per model sold; and, Infiniti spent $1,861 per

model sold. By contrast, Mercedes-Benz and BMW spent $941 and $451, respectively, on measured media per model they sold in the U.S. (For more, go to kantarmedia.us and type into the search field, "Automotive Adage Report.")

11. The geographical term "first world" refers to so-called developed capitalist countries. The term has been falling from grace for being elitist and shortsighted. (Jared Diamond's quote is from *Collapse: How Societies Choose to Fail or Succeed*.)

12. "If Americans want to live the American Dream, they should go to Denmark," says economist Richard Wilkinson. But learning to speak Danish is notoriously difficult. (Catherine Rampell, "Fatalism and the American Dream," in *The New York Times*. Nov. 23, 2011.)

13. In my study, 18 percent of Southerners, Northeasterners, and Midwesterners said they no longer have an American Dream versus 20 percent of West Coasters. But if Californians are excluded from the West's tally, those without a dream falls to 16 percent. Meanwhile, across the nation, 21 percent of men compared to 16 percent of women answered, "I don't have an American Dream."

14. Land in the U.S. used to be so cheap. In 1803, the United States government paid France roughly four cents an acre to purchase the Louisiana Territory. That's about 85 cents an acre in today's money. (To convert dollar amounts from yesteryear to now, visit oregonstate.edu and type "inflation conversion factors" into the search field.)

15. For over 15 years, MasterCard's "Priceless" campaign with its slogan, "There are some things money can't buy. For everything else there's MasterCard®," has shifted consumers' attitudes toward credit cards and credit-card holders. When credit cards were introduced, credit-card holders were often seen as slutty spenders prone to APR hangovers that no Egg McMuffin or breakfast taco can cure. These days, church ministers swipe them, and their benefits, like their ease of use,

are cited over their downsides. This attitudinal shift wasn't cheap. MasterCard has spent hundreds of millions of dollars on ads in the U.S. to position itself as the card for upstanding citizens with self-control, who appreciate that money has less value than what matters most. Tangent: Why do athletes often appear in ads for credit cards? They exemplify the virtue of self-control.

16. In my study, before citizens answered how much extra cash it would take for them to feel more content, they were primed with: *"During the previous 12 months, think about the amount of money that you've spent on your lifestyle."* A different primer would have given different results.

17. For centuries, money and power have helped men to bed women. Laura Betzig calculated that in early history, emperors often had thousands of concubines or wives; princes, hundreds; upper-class men, up to a dozen; and middle-class men, three to four. (Laura Betzig, *Despotism and Differential Reproduction: A Darwinian View of History*, as discussed in Steven Pinker, *The Better Angels of Our Nature*.)

18. In 2012, U.S. median household incomes ranged from an estimated $37,095 in Mississippi to $71,122 in Maryland. Meanwhile, the federal minimum wage was $15,080 per annum. However, some states set their own minimum wages, in which case, employees are entitled to the higher rate. (American Community Survey, 2012; dol.gov.)

19. In my study, out of the age cohorts, 45- to 65-year-olds (on average) wanted the most extra cash to feel more content, partly because many of them must decide: "What will I fund: my parents' elder care, my kids' college, or my retirement?"

20. According to a December 2007 Gallup poll, 46 percent of Americans had bought a state lottery ticket in the preceding 12 months.

21. When I asked Americans, *"In life, what's the best way to get money?"* 74 percent said, "Earn it," 13 percent said, "Win it," 9 percent, "Inherit it," 3 percent "Marry it," and less than 1 percent said, "Borrow it." Tangent: Most of the "marry it" group seemed to view marriage as a gateway to a long-term loving relationship with a generous partner, rather than a fast track into a cushy divorce settlement. The "marry it" group was comprised roughly of 50 percent women and 50 percent men.

22. Many animals, including birds, monkeys, and rats seem to prefer earning food to receiving handouts. In the 1960s, scientists placed 200 rats inside Skinner boxes, wherein each rat could decide how it'd receive food while in captivity. Each rat could either 1) press a bar that released food pellets, or 2) ignore the bar and simply gobble pellets out of a pre-filled bowl. 199 rats pressed the bar. (Glen Jensen, "Preference for Bar Pressing Over "Freeloading" as a Function of Number of Rewarded Presses," *Journal of Experimental Psychology*, 1963; 65:451–454.)

23. America's celebration of the self-made man stems from factors such as the legacy of the Protestant work ethic and the influence of the Horatio Alger myth. For more, check out Max Weber, *The Protestant Ethic and the Spirit of Capitalism*.

24. In my study, one likely reason why men (on average) asked for more additional money to feel more content than did women, is that men (on average) currently possess more earning power in the labor market (bls.gov). Plus, at this moment in time, men often covet more expensive vehicles.

CHAPTER THREE

Work

"Time is an illusion. Lunchtime doubly so."

—Douglas Adams

In the late 1960s, when my father began his advertising career, he assumed the profession would grant him a life of fast cars, flash money, and fabulous women (call him Bond, Mr. I'm-in-advertising Bond), while some of his mates went into it for its then-notorious boozy lunches. In the end, my dad and his buds got much of what they wanted (hangovers notwithstanding). Today, advertising is a career for masochists. Weekends are "work-ends." Salaries, stagnant. Vacations, paltry. And the marketing-jargon in the air is thicker than Beijing's smog. No wonder, it's a young person's game. Although, #FarWorseIndustriesExist. And these are #FirstWorldProblems. So don't feel sorry for me; I work with wildly creative people. And I get to pitch. (No relation to a baseball diamond.) Because pitching, as you probably know, is when a client invites several agencies to devise and present campaigns on one of their brands (for free!) for the chance to be crowned their agency partner.

For a planner like me, the start to a pitch goes somewhat like this: 1) sit with the client, and listen to their goals, 2) soak brain in caffeine, 3) conduct consumer research, 4) share findings with teammates, and 5) impersonate Russell Crowe in *Gladiator* by roaring at the creative department, "Unleash hell. Go make some ads!" (Cue gnashing of teeth, swords on shields, and the death rattle of our opponents' ideas being crushed underfoot.)[1]

But if I had my life over, I might not be a planner. Because, while pitching allows me to solve puzzles while nurturing creatives to produce their best work, I'm arguably better suited to manning medieval catapults (making the *Gladiator* reference apt), because I'm built like an Amazon and I hate sitting still. (If you see a vacancy for a catapultress on Monster.com, email me.)

Yes, the relationships we have with our work are ever-changing and complex. But if you're in the business of selling, you must know what jobs people do for a living and how they feel about them. Because the work we do, and our expectations of the labor market influences our psychology, biology, and our environment (and vice versa)—from how we (and other consumers) construct our identities, to how we think others perceive us, to how we spend our days, to the media we consume and the content we share, to the goods we commonly buy. This information helps creatives make ads that resonate with their respective target audiences, while it also helps media planners and buyers place ads in physical, digital, and broadcast properties frequented by their target audiences. That's why I'm a huge fan of gathering occupational data. By the end of this chapter, I'm hoping you'll want to slip on an "I ♥ Occupational Data" jersey too.

Career Advice for the Ambitious

Over the last 60 years, employee contentment in the United States has steadily fallen, even though it's common knowledge when choosing a career to pursue, a person should consider her or his:

- Interests

- Preferred salary range (modest to big bucks)

- Signature strengths,[2] and

- Appetite for challenges that allow them to grow

That last point is key, because as psychologist Mihaly Csikszentmihalyi (pronounced CHEEK-sent-me-hi-ee) says, "[Our] best moments usually occur when . . . [our] body or mind is stretched to its limits in a voluntary effort to accomplish something difficult and worthwhile."[3]

In addition, it's often worth pursuing careers that have been matched to your personality type. Although to paraphrase Whitman: people are large; they contain multitudes. The suggestions dished out by psychometric tests, like the Myers-Briggs Type Indicator, can be hilariously inappropriate and/or woefully underpaying.[4] (My recommendations included writer and musician, both of which usually require loans from the Bank of Mom and Dad.)

Yet, even when job seekers embrace the edict of "do what you are," landing and keeping your job-match ain't easy. The U.S. economy's a yo-yo dieter: it booms and crashes. And, contrary to the occupations commonly seen on U.S. TV, like model-slash-cop and brooding -but-sexy surgeon, in the nonfictional world, the country's largest occupations are retail-sales worker positions (in which over eight million Americans are employed) followed by server positions (in which over six million Americans are employed).[5] This may shock the roughly 150 million non-U.S. adults who expressed interest in migrating here in recent Gallup polls.[6]

So, if the American Dream demands a good job with decent pay, what's a person to do? Let's hear from the people.

School's Out for Summer

When I asked Americans to imagine themselves as careers counselors tasked with advising teens on professions offering a livable steady-ish wage, 10 percent said, "Who cares? There are no jobs" or "No career is one-size-fits-all." (That last one's true.)

The rest came up with a shortlist of jobs some teens might want to do. The occupations chosen reflects our era: manufacturing was absent; ditto, selling encyclopedias door-to-door; and not even Floridians living near Cape Canaveral said, "Astronaut." (Sorry, NASA.)

Practical Jobs for the Near Future (in order of most recommended)

1. Healthcare (with shout-outs for geriatric care and addiction counseling)
2. Information technology/video-game designer
3. Teacher/professor
4. Engineer (specializing in renewable energy)
5. Lawyer (focusing on divorce law)

6. Homeland security/police/armed forces

7. Entrepreneur

8. Farmer (with marijuana, one suggested cash crop)

9. Financier/stock-market whiz[7]

There were stipulations attached. Teachers, some warned, get frustrated teaching "to the test." Doctors, others said, fear they might get sued. And only 18 percent of my self-employed respondents recommended entrepreneurship due to the number of nights they'd spent staring at the ceiling thinking, "Will I earn enough this month to keep the lights on, pay my employees, and pay myself?" which is a far cry from the be-your-own-boss fantasy of raking in cash, taking orders from no one, and cultivating one's hair into a style rivaling "The Anna Wintour" or "The Donald Trump."

However, such job pitfalls were primarily voiced to urge teens to get real, not glum about the labor market. To paraphrase one Texan respondent: "Careers are tough. Pace yourself. Burn out early and you might miss something astounding." Other words of wisdom from my surveys included:

- Master your profession's basics on the job, in college, or at trade school

- Aim to make your colleagues think you are the best thing that ever happened to them, or risk losing your employment to another person or machine

- Psychoanalyze your boss. Some will want you to achieve greatness. Others will want you to parrot

back what they say. But even ones nicknamed
Darth Vader will teach you a thing or two, before
you go elsewhere[8]

- Rein in your ego, and

- Leave racy garments like bottomless chaps at home,
  unless your occupation thrives on being theatrical,
  like tattoo artists

Social scientists would agree: in regards to clothing, studies have shown that strangers take, on average, one-tenth of a second or less to evaluate us.[9] If they assess us to be high in status, they more often listen to our opinions.[10] Consequently, how we dress for work matters to our careers and the careers of any boss we represent. And in terms of egos, many young adults fall prey to the Dunning-Kruger effect, wherein the unskilled don't know they're unskilled, resulting in overconfidence and annoying (but also amusing) bouts of know-it-all-itis.[11]

But considering how savvy Americans are about the job market, what percentage of them like their jobs?

The Secrets to a Happy Worklife

When I asked full-time American employees how they feel about their current jobs, 40 percent said, "I enjoy my job"; 20 percent said, "It's okay"; 20 percent said, "I do it for the money"; 10 percent wanted to switch companies; and the rest yearned for a reinvention—to spread their wings in a whole new career.[12] However, among those who said, "I enjoy my job," many added, "Because I have one." This suggests that in competitive labor markets, the word enjoy can imply, "I wake up excited to go to work" to "I'd rather stay at home." But the following quotes are from employees who appeared fairly satisfied with their day-to-day:

> *"I work in the fields. There is a beginning. The hay is ready to be cut. Next, there's the baling. And then, there's moving hay to another location. You look back . . . and see completeness."*
> —From Colorado, age 52

> *"I train bomb- and drug-sniffing dogs for the police. In this age of machines, nothing beats them. Age has slowed me down . . . [but I like figuring out] ways to train them to help people."*
> —From New Mexico, age 47

And:

> *"I work with special-needs children, though I'm on a parenting break. Most of the time the difference I make is minimal. Although once in a while, I see a breakthrough."*
> —From California, age 28

In addition to the jobs featured above (farmer, animal trainer, teacher), other occupations in which Americans often seemed to be fairly content at work included: historian, genealogist, home restorer, classic-car mechanic, park ranger, gardener, nurse, psychologist, photographer, librarian, and scientist. As well as other jobs in which employees said that, while at work, they're somewhat able to (psst, here come the secrets to a happy worklife culled from my respondents' answers):

- Prioritize and complete tasks in the manner of their choosing

- Stretch their minds and *limbs*. As economist Robert Frank explains, "[In the late '80s] newly constructed office buildings allowed an average of 250 square feet of space per worker, including a proportionate share of the building's lobby, corridors, and restrooms. . . . [A decade later] customer-service telephone operators typically receive 100 square feet or less"[13]

- See an outcome to their labors (tricky to do in corporations), and

- Live up to Aristotle's "purposeful life" (a.k.a., "do good, feel good"), whereby what they get up to at work (and how they interpret their actions) makes them feel more connected to others, their heritage, and/or the land, providing them with a sense of belonging to this hectic world through good times and bad[14]

In summary, people in my study who enjoyed their work often felt a sense of autonomy, personal growth, and a belief that their actions mattered.[15] Whereas, full-time employees who'd rated their jobs as okay or lower had more often said:

- "I've been disrespected at work"[16]

- "When I get asked what I do for a living, it makes me feel terrible," and

- "If I were rich, I would tell my boss to stick it," with men aged 35-49, the most likely to have dreamt of their boss's demise (This reminds me of Caesar saying *"Et tu, Brute?"* Note to self: togas to be banned at the next office party.)[17]

Okay, so now that Americans have: 1) spilled their secrets to a happy worklife, and 2) given us a shortlist of recommended jobs, how do you get one of these jobs?

Do You Trust Me?

Trusting others often feels unnatural. For example, do you trust me? Of course not. I'm an account planner; a Scot (who gets accused of speaking in tongues, whenever I say "Aye right." Translation: "I don't believe it." Scots are a cynical bunch); and, we've only known each other three chapters. I wouldn't trust me either. Nor would I expect a potential employer to trust me if all she or he had to go on was my resume, because:

- Everyone knows resumes get inflated (When I asked Americans whether they'd rat on a coworker who'd lied on their resume, 56 percent of my full-time employed respondents said no, partly because, as one summed up, "Everyone's at it.")[18]

- Educational credentials (even when genuine) are almost impossible to evaluate unless the hirer went to the same school and studied the same thing, and

- Trusting strangers is not instinctive to us; it opposes our species' psychological priming for control, thus the cliché, "Trust must be earned"[19]

This brings us to arguably *the* most important career advice Americans had for teens:

> *"To get ahead in life, look to your family, their trade, their connections. Then look elsewhere."*
>
> —From Georgia, age 75

That's because even in America—a land with no Queen (except Dairy Queen), or Posh Spice (she's back in Blighty)—success often rests on who you know.[20] Hence, the popularity of business networking events and sites, such as LinkedIn that offers job seekers a chance to schmooze with bigwigs in the hope one of them will commend them to the powers that be, giving them a toehold onto the ladder of a desirable industry.[21] Then, with fortune and fortitude, that person might get to the top. You do it, America. It can be done!

But if you've yet to get your break, remember this: 1) challenges can be found in your hobbies; 2) if you think your job's lousy, think of the jobs your ancestors had (one of my grandmothers was a live-in servant. For her daily breakfast, m'lady would allot her one-half of a boiled egg); 3) many award winners still feel unsuccessful; and 4) when I asked Americans, *"When a person asks what you do for a living, how do you feel as you answer?"* those happiest answering that question were not people who currently enjoy their jobs. But the retired, who having weathered the "if-onlys," heartache, and "what ifs" of the labor market, can now look back on their careers and see it for the friendships, the pride in a job well done, and the knowledge they survived it.

End of Chapter Sidebar: Stay-At-Home Parents

In the 1960s, Betty Friedan cautioned women against the hellish pointlessness of the "housewife trap" in her bestseller, *The Feminine Mystique*. Today, social scientists possess more information to suggest job satisfaction is possible at work, at home, and at both, depending on (and this is crucial) an individual's temperament, well-being, and their environment.[22] However, when I asked stay-at-home parents, *"When a person asks what you do for a living, how do you feel as you answer?"* they (as a group) were not as happy answering that question as the retired.[23]

Brain Fuel: If You Study/Work in Advertising

Name four signature strengths of the agency you work at, or the university you attend. (A list of all 24 signature strengths is available at the second endnote of this chapter.)

Name four signature strengths of one of your favorite brands.

Think of another of your favorite brands. Name an occupation its consumers often work in. Now, name three products commonly bought by people in that occupation.

How does your job help you to live up to Aristotle's "purposeful life" a.k.a., "do good, feel good"?

Name three tactics your agency/university uses to build trust between itself and its prospective clients/students.

Brain Fuel: If You Study/Work in Marketing

Think of one of your favorite brands. Name four of its signature strengths. (For a list of all 24 signature strengths, visit the second endnote of this chapter.)

Think of another of your favorite brands. How does this brand help its consumers live up to Aristotle's "purposeful life" a.k.a., "do good, feel good"?

The market research firm Harris Interactive conducts annual polls on the reputations of the 100 most-visible companies among the U.S. public. The results of these polls can be found by Googling "Harris poll reputation quotient." Once you've found the most recent top 100, pick one high performer and research probable reasons behind the public's high trustworthiness of that company.

Fieldwork for All

Sign up for a cooking or art class on Groupon.com to remember how good it feels to take home an outcome of your labors.

Visit a café for 30 minutes to observe how many customers are polite toward the employees versus how many are rude. Write down what happens during a friendly customer-employee exchange. Think about the tone of voice and body language of these individuals: from the shape of their lips, to the positions of their hips, to the tension in their shoulders. Next, read Paul Ekman's *Emotions Revealed: Recognizing Faces and Feelings to Improve Communication and Emotional Life.*

Roam your neighborhood or the Internet to observe how businesses seek to gain your trust. For example, doctors frame their credentials inside their consulting rooms, restaurants hang sanitation letter-grades inside their windows, and online businesses feature customer reviews on their websites.

Notes

1. Agencies with the best ideas don't always win pitches(!) Clients consider many factors when deciding who'll get their business, such as an agency's fee structure, geographical location, and track record in making ads in their category.

2. Psychologist Martin Seligman believes humans possess 24 signature strengths: appreciation, bravery, caution, creativity, curiosity, enthusiasm, fairness, forgiveness, gratitude, humility, humor, integrity, intimacy, judgment, kindness, leadership, love of learning, optimism, perseverance, perspective, sense of responsibility, self-control, sociability, and spirituality. To improve your overall subjective well-being, Seligman recommends identifying four or more of your strongest strengths, and using them daily. (Martin Seligman, *Authentic Happiness.*)

3. Mihaly Csikszentmihalyi's quote is from *Flow: The Psychology of Optimal Experience.*

4. As professor Robert Todd Carroll explains, "Providing personality tests and profiles has become a kind of entertainment on the Internet. [But] there is also a pernicious side to these profiles: they can lead to discrimination and poor career counseling." That's partly because one popular test, the Myers-Briggs Type Indicator (MBTI), perpetuates the myth that introversion and extroversion exist on either sides of a linear scale. In plain English, the MBTI suggests extroverts act like extroverts in every kind of social situation, while introverts act like introverts in every kind of social situation, even though, ever since the 1920s, evidence gathered by psychologist Theodore Newcomb debunked this theory. (Robert Carroll, *The Skeptic's Dictionary: A Collection of Strange Beliefs, Amusing Deceptions, and Dangerous Delusions;* Jonathan Baron, *Thinking and Deciding.*)

5. The three largest occupational groups in the U.S. are office and administrative support (over 21 million employees), sales (over 13.5 million employees), and food preparation and serving (over 11.5 million employees). (bls.gov, May 2012 figures.)

6. The Holmes and Rahe Stress Scale estimates an individual's risk of illness from stressful events. The more "life change units" that a person clocks up in any given year, the more likely they are to fall ill. On the scale, imprisonment equals 63 units, while migrating to a different country isn't featured, but events associated with it are like changes in: residence (20 units), number of family reunions (15 units), living conditions (25 units), social activities (18 units), and working conditions (20 units), totaling 98 units. (Thomas H. Holmes and Richard H. Rahe, "The Social Readjustment Rating Scale," *Journal of Psychosomatic Research*, 1967; 11(2):213–218; in this chapter, the cited number of people who fancy migrating to the U.S. is based on rolling averages from Gallup polls conducted between 2009 and 2011. gallup.com.)

7. In my study, other practical careers recommended to high schoolers included: dietician, smartphone designer, air-conditioning installer, and member of the criminal classes. Less than one percent recommended a career in advertising. More recommended a career in adult entertainment(!)

8. Top executives are four times more likely to be psychopaths than the general public, explains psychologist Oliver James. But even bosses who start off good-natured can turn rotten. As professor Robert Trivers explains, ". . . Psychologists have shown that power corrupts our mental processes almost at once. When a feeling of power is induced in people, they are less likely to take others' viewpoint and more likely to center their thinking on themselves. The result is a reduced ability to comprehend how others see, think, and feel." (Oliver James, *Office Politics*; Robert Trivers, *The Folly of Fools*.)

9. Everyone judges a book by its cover. But how accurately do we assess strangers? Psychologist Frank Bernieri believes that when we meet someone that person's "personality is truthfully encoded within the first 30 seconds of behavior." But factors such as the person's charisma and our level of social intelligence clouds our judgment. (Janine Willis and Alexander Todorov, "First Impressions: Making Up Your Mind After a 100-Ms Exposure to a Face," *Psychological Science*, 2006; 17(7):592–598; Frank Bernieri's quote is from Lea Winerman, "Thin Slices of Life," *American Psychological Association*, 2005; 36(3):54.)

10. According to psychologists Ivan Kelly and D. Dickson, we more often accept unfavorable assessments of our personalities, "when delivered by people with high perceived status," as opposed to being delivered by people with low perceived status. As we gain life experience, this bias lessens. (D. H. Dickson and I. W. Kelly, "The 'Barnum Effect' in Personality Assessment: A Review of the Literature," *Psychological Reports*, 1985; 57:367–382.)

11. For more on the Dunning-Kruger effect, read Justin Kruger and David Dunning, "Unskilled and Unaware of It: How Difficulties in Recognizing One's Own Incompetence Lead to Inflated Self-Assessments," *Psychology*, 2009; 1:30–46.

12. In my study, when I asked employees who wanted to switch companies, *"What is your main motivation for wanting to change jobs?"* their top answer was *"I want more money,"* followed by *"I want to be treated with more respect."*

13. Robert Frank's quote is from *Luxury Fever*.

14. How we interpret our actions influences our psychological well-being. If you've begun to question the utility of your actions, read Aaron T. Beck, *Cognitive Therapy and the Emotional Disorders*.

15. As behavioral economist Dan Ariely says, "Maybe we need the illusion that our work might one day matter to many people. That it might be of some value in the big, broad world out there (we might call this Meaning with a large M)? . . . But fundamentally, I think that almost any aspect of meaning (even small-m meaning) can be sufficient to drive our behavior." In other words, every job—from puppeteer to pastry chef—has the potential to be a calling. (Dan Ariely, *The Upside of Irrationality: The Unexpected Benefits of Defying Logic at Work and at Home*.)

16. If you've been insulted at work, you're not alone. In my study, 45 percent of full-time employees who rated their jobs as okay said they have been disrespected at work, compared to 40 percent of full-time employees who said they enjoy their jobs.

17. If you're a boss, the person daydreaming of your demise is likely your second-in-command. Why? Familiarity breeds contempt and seconds-in-command usually have the most to gain when the top dog topples. This suggests Karl Marx was rallying the wrong crowd when he said, "Workers of the world unite; you have nothing to lose but your chains." Throughout history, it's been seconds-in-command, not the poor, who've spearheaded bloody and bloodless coups. The poor typically lack the resources to knock the world upside down. Plus, they're usually focused on their daily survival.

18. Scientists recently found "substantial misstatements" on roughly 400 out of 1,000 resumes. This practice strengthens "who you know" as the qualifier for landing good jobs in America, which is problematic for folks with thin "social capital." (Jeffery Pfeffer, *What Were They Thinking? Unconventional Wisdom about Management*.)

19. Exercising good manners and self-restraint are also not instinctive to us. (Norbert Elias, *The Civilizing Process*.)

20. According to social scientists, children from low-income families in America have marginally higher social mobility compared to those in the U.K, but less so than children in Denmark, Austria, Norway, Finland, Canada, Sweden, Germany, Spain, and France. (OECD, *Economic Policy Reforms: Going for Growth 2010*.)

21. In 2011 in the U.S., immigrants started 28 percent of new businesses, despite accounting for 13 percent of the population. In other words, these immigrants leaned out of the labor market. Those "leaning in"—to borrow Facebook COO Sheryl Sandberg's terminology—were often keen networkers. When I asked 18- to 59-year-old Americans, *"At social events, what do you usually ask strangers about?"* roughly 60 percent of naturalized citizens compared to roughly 50 percent of U.S.-born citizens said, "Their occupation." (Robert Fairlie, *"Open for Business: How Immigrants Are Driving Small Business Creation in the United States*," August 2012, renewoureconomy.org/research.)

22. Betty Friedan's quote from *The Feminine Mystique* is "Women who do not look for jobs equal to their actual capacity, who do not let themselves develop the lifetime interests and goals which require serious education and training, who take a job at twenty or forty to 'help out at home' or just to kill extra time, are walking, almost as surely as the ones who stay inside the housewife trap, to a non-existent future."

23. For more on shifting societal perceptions toward homemakers, read Stephanie Coontz, *Marriage, a History: How Love Conquered Marriage*.

CHAPTER FOUR

Beauty

*"Mirror, mirror, on the wall, who in this
land is fairest of all?"*
—The Brothers Grimm, "Little Snow-White"

When brothers John and Thomas Knoll invented Photoshop in 1988, neither could've foretold that one day their image-processing platform would be used to expand thigh-gaps on models intensifying the public's backlash against the media for promoting unnatural body types as desirable.[1] "We knew we had a groundbreaking technology on our hands," Thomas said, "but we never anticipated how much it would impact the images we see all around us."[2]

Oh, Photoshop. Agencies use it. Consumers use it too, especially on match.com (suggested slogan: "You looked different in your profile." "So did you"). But, regardless of whether you're selling skinny jeans or your sexy self (*wink*), it pays to remember the difference between telling people white lies versus whoppers. White lies, once uncovered, tend to be forgiven by others—accepted as mere showmanship. Whereas whoppers, once uncovered, are typically met with consumers' exasperation or ire.[3] Yet one exception to this rule involves skincare, in which some consumers prefer ads in which wrinkles have been erased with the ardor of a fevered Dorian Gray. Why? You're about to find out more about advertising's sliding scale of "lies."

Under the Skin

If humans were rational (which would be a dull state of consumer affairs), the global $100 billion-plus "anti-aging" beauty market would adhere to the following rules:[4]

- Creams costing $200 per oz. would be more potent than cheaper ones

- The term "anti-aging" would be exiled for being ageist

- Extreme airbrushing would go the way of the dodo, and

- Purported product benefits would rely on major research, rather than on half-assed experiments better suited to an era when leeches were deemed cutting-edge medical treatments

But as you know, luxury creams are often no more effective than drugstore brands. The term "anti-aging" pops-up on products manufactured by companies whose hiring policies state, "We don't discriminate on the basis of age." Spokespersons for lotions often resemble statues: their faces so manipulated, they're incapable of expressing emotion. And according to the American Academy of Dermatology, the oft-used phrase "clinically proven" simply means a product "was given to consumers to try. It doesn't mean the product underwent clinical trials" or that it's been approved by the FDA.[5]

While another seemingly irrational side to the skincare industry is the steeper a product's price, the grander its cock-and-bull story. Take for instance, this description for a moisturizer costing almost one grand per 8.5 oz. tub:

> "*Born from the sea, the legendary Crème de la Mer has the power to transform the skin. In a short time . . .skin looks virtually ageless. . . . The secret to activating [this nutrient-rich Miracle Broth™] lies in a soothing ritual. Crème de la Mer must be warmed for a few seconds between the fingers until it becomes translucent, then pressed gently into the skin.*"
>
> —Cremedelamer.com

Legend. Miracle. Ritual. La Mer's website reads like Dan Brown.[6]

Yet when I planned advertising strategies for high-end skincare products, my attempt to inject less (ahem) hogwash into the category failed. As I'd wrongly assumed my client's target audience (35- to 50-year-old women who in the last year had spent over $500 on youth-bestowing lotions) would appreciate ads in which the spokes-person looked somewhat human and the copy in the ads were more straight shootin'. Yet in focus groups for the brand, the mocked-up ads favored by the target audience featured:

- The most mannequin-looking photos of our spokesperson

- Gossipy copy, such as "Hi there, wanna know a secret?" and

- Our client's most expensive product haloed under light as though the product's properties rivaled those of the Holy Grail[7]

I sat there stumped. I needed a clue. After sixty minutes of listening to these intelligent women, I pointed to their favorite ad and blurted, "But the model—she's so airbrushed. There's no skin to see."

"But she's flawless," said one of them.

"But . . ."

"Shh," said another, clasping my hands. She literally disarmed me!

Then it clicked: these ladies didn't want me bleating on about facts. They didn't want me droning on about the relationship between healthy skin, eating a balanced diet, and the diligent application of sunscreen. Nor did they want me leading them in a discussion on how to tame the demons inside their heads that taunted "Must. Be. Perfect." Today, it was miracles they'd wanted—instant fixes to life's indignities. To believe that somewhere out there existed a cream that when they applied it 1) their faces would be reborn, unmarked by disappointment, and 2) their inner "Lady Peaceful, Lady Happy" would reawaken, never to leave their side. They didn't give a hoot that my client's products were arguably slightly better than its competitor brands. Not at those prices. They wanted to pretend the products themselves were almost supernatural. They wanted Dan Brown. No surprise, the focus groups had been in Los Angeles, a city where beauty-standards for women (and men) have been stratospherically skewed by its glut of models-slash-actresses with dermatologists on speed dial.

And so, the hyper-airbrushed ads ran. After which the client left us for a firm in New York specializing in high-end fashion ads starring (you've guessed it) computer-generated thigh-gaps. For us, getting dumped was not that dreadful. Because, despite the pleasures we'd taken in the thoughtfully-crafted scents, textures, and packaging of our client's goods 1) we'd disliked peddling whoppers to the target audience—even though, arguably, they were in on the ruse, and 2) in terms of presenting women as mannequins, well . . . those waxworks at Tussauds aren't attractive, they're *attractions*. And yes, they don't feel pain. But they don't feel. Period. And where's the joy in that?[8]

Once Upon a Time

In the United States, elixirs touting miraculous effects have done a roaring trade ever since medicine shows with their horse-drawn wagons pulled up to attract roadside crowds.[9] And while these snake-oil salesmen with their colorful tales duped many a pioneer, it's now common knowledge that miracle-touted items (e.g., Miracle Whip) don't beget marvels (although they can make you a delicious coleslaw). Yet many folks, myself included, still splurge on, or regularly buy miracle skincare-products thanks to its:

- Bathroom-shelf appeal

- Treat-myself appeal, and/or

- Fantasy appeal that accounts for much of the price gap between luxury- as opposed to budget-brands[10]

Speaking of fantasy, one tale commonly spun by high-end skincare-ads is "This product will give you youthful beauty" that some folks associate with the narrative: youthful beauty marries money, gets a mansion, gets a clothing allowance, gets a walk-in closet, gets a larger mansion, she lives happily ever after.

Or does she?[11] Because:

- Beauty is no guarantee against torment (Google "Whitney Houston life")

- Falling in love is not restricted to the young and symmetrical (contrary to plots of many a rom-com movie), and

- Walk-in closets are overrated unless they open to Narnia (some of my friends would disagree)

In addition, many high-end skincare-ads feed into beauty myths that many of us have been taught from a tender age that—should we try to live up to—seldom make us happy. For example, many girls continue to be fed mission-statements along the lines of "For your dreams to come true: look forever 20-something." While boys more often get: "For success in life, why not model your body after Michelangelo's David: your mane to be luscious as Samson's, and your muscles to be rock hard."

That's why "get gorgeous" products for guys often declare war against baldness or puniness, rather than promising the user, instant weight loss or baby-soft skin.[12] Psst! Men use anti-wrinkle creams too, their fingers leaving scoop-marks inside delicate pots often belonging to girlfriends or wives: a clunky habit that's led many a skincare firm to repackage its women's products into opaque pump-dispensing bottles to help guys better pilfer.[13]

But men's moisturized fingers aside, the beauty industry's long-game involves snagging disposable dollars from women, not men. One reason why is that female-oriented beauty/grooming products, as opposed to those aimed at guys, have often raked in prettier profits: in part, because their marketing efforts have often made better use of illusion-boosting tactics, for example:

- Women *and men* look elsewhere as their fantasies wane.[14] High-end women's skincare companies know this. That's why to sustain their profits, they rely heavily on gifts-with-purchase, loyalty programs, and their rapid innovation cycles, and

- The five senses feed our imagination. That's why hair-thickening shampoos marketed at women look, lather, and smell luxurious. However, unfortunately for Rogaine (a hair restorer for limp locks first marketed to men), at its launch, it smelled banal (when it could've smelled of whisky—so rugged, follicles would've wanted to hit the deck for one-armed pushups). And its exterior left much to be desired as well, as the cardboard box it came in resembled those for medium-flow tampons that, on drugstore shelves, aren't exactly a siren's song to chaps with male pattern baldness[15]

But, despite Rogaine's checkered fortunes, hair-rejuvenating products for men and women remains a goldmine thanks to factors, such as 1) the number of youth-centric workplaces in the U.S., 2) the plethora of divorcées dating online, and 3) the unjust reality that youthful beauty has its perks, such as receiving clemency for wrong-doings.[16] For example, in one famous social-psychology experiment, a mock jury displayed greater leniency toward defendants whom they regarded as attractive than those they deemed less so.[17]

Talking of getting away with things: here's a mischievous tangent . . .

L'Oréal is a pro at being forgiven for being naughty, as the multi-billion-dollar company receives major slack from consumers and watchdogs whenever it's outed for advertising its shampoos and mascaras on models wearing hair or lash extensions. One reason for the goodwill shown toward the company is its tagline, "Because you're worth it." As in the words of business theorist Jeffrey Pfeffer, "[When] you compliment someone, that person owes you something in return just as surely as if you had bought the individual dinner or given a gift." Consequently, when L'Oréal's exposed for playing loose with the truth, its actions are generally absolved by the public, reasserting the axiom that flattery pays when it's done well.[18] (P.S. You're gorgeous.)

Okay, now a question for you. What percentage of Americans love their looks, considering the billions of dollars' worth of beauty products sold annually in the U.S.? It must be almost everyone, right?

Hot or Not

In 1973, psychologist Beulah Amsterdam wanted to know whether babies recognized themselves in the mirror. To explore this riddle, he used the rouge test: 1) put rouge on baby's nose, 2) place clown before mirror, and 3) observe. Babies aged six- to twelve-months typically think, "Another baby. Let's play." Infants in their second year of life are usually wary of the imposter, before turning away. While toddlers aged 24-months usually know it's themselves, prompting some to smear off the rouge, while others are too busy thinking, "Where's my juice box?"[19]

But when you and I see our reflections, it reminds us of 1) our mortality, 2) how well we've been treating our bodies (perhaps too well), and 3) how our appearance compares to that of others. Because, in the words of economist Robert Frank, "[Humans] have strong concerns about relative position"—a phenomenon resulting in websites like Hot or Not, where people get ranked as though they were chili sauce.[20] (Reading this book makes you hot!)

However, whom we choose to compare ourselves to, and the evaluations we give to ourselves and others is influenced by the big three: our biology, psychology, and our environment. For example, when cheerful, we more often compare ourselves favorably against Mr. or Ms. Average versus rating ourselves unfavorably next to Mr. or Ms. Model; while environmental changes, such as installing soft lighting, can silence our inner critics—a truism that inspired Virgin America's design director to install low-wattage bulbs, as opposed to fluorescents, inside the airline's toilets. But (nosy as always) when I asked Americans, *"How did you respond to your wake-up reflection last week?"* a mere 13 percent said they'd been "Looking good."[21] (Hey, interior decorators. Public service announcement: mood lighting is needed in homes!)

But what else did Americans have to say about their mirror image?

"How Did You Respond to Your Wake-Up Reflection Last Week?"

	PERCENTAGE OF WOMEN WHO'D THOUGHT THIS	PERCENTAGE OF MEN WHO'D THOUGHT THIS
I look tired	48	32
Clean face and teeth? Check	33	34
Bad hair/gray hair/no hair	24	27
Have I put on weight?	25	19
Wrinkles[22]	20	9
I look like mom/dad	11	5
Looking good[23]	10	16
I know I'm younger	10	6
Too depressed to look	3	4

(Columns add up to more than 100 percent.
Respondents were able to choose multiple answers.)

As seen in the table, more women than men mentioned their wrinkles or weight, while a smidgen more guys focused on their hair (these gaps both widened with age).[24] But the big yawn between the sexes was: 48 percent of women versus 32 percent of men believed they'd looked tired. That's *a lot* of people. And it's this fatigue, especially among women, that's arguably draining the nation's vitality faster than the sight of crows' feet, ample thighs, and shifting hairlines. Because tiredness, as you'll well know, isn't a joke: it makes us more self-critical, damaging our emotional well-being and the moods of those around us; while it also hampers our ability to juggle stress and complete goals that help define who we are. Thankfully, there are things we can do.[25]

Operation Goodnight

In the 1970s, America's energy crisis involved oil. Today, it's people, with folks often worn out despite constant access to stimulants like coffee.[26] But why are women, rather than men, apparently more in need of Zzz's? (It's not that women are feeble; childbirth is not for wimps.) One likely culprit in this crisis involves uneven dynamics in personal relationships. Because (spoiler alert!) in my study, 18- to 44-year-old single women without kids reported fairly similar levels of "I look tired (in the mirror)" compared to 18- to 44-year-old single men without kids. Not so for those married or cohabiting:

America's Energy Crisis
(Recent Thoughts While Looking in the Mirror)

RELATIONSHIP/ PARENTAL STATUS	PERCENTAGE OF WOMEN, AGE 18–44, WHO'D THOUGHT, "I LOOK TIRED"	PERCENTAGE OF MEN, AGE 18–44, WHO'D THOUGHT, "I LOOK TIRED"
Single, no kids[27]	46	42
Married/cohabiting, no kids	59	28*
Married/cohabiting, kids[28]	59	34

* = Small sample size

Now I'm not here bashing matrimony or cohabitation, because as psychologist Martin Seligman explains, "The jury is still out on what causes the proven fact that married people are happier than unmarried people."[29] Yet as psychologist Daniel Gilbert clarifies, *"It's not marriage that makes you happy, it's happy marriage that makes you happy."*[30]

To which I'll add, in my study, solo-living Director-women (for whom, work often keeps them occupied), and Explorer-women and Explorer-men (for whom, their many interests can provide them with contentment), in general, reported being as happy, if not slightly happier, with their lives over the past year, when compared to married or cohabiting peers of the same personality type.

Furthermore, even though married or cohabiting Negotiators and Builders (of both sexes) did appear (on average) to be slightly happier with their recent lives, when compared to Negotiators and Builders in my study who had been living solo, the happiness gaps between these groups weren't massive. Because, despite marriage's potential social and financial benefits, marriage is compromise.[31] Therefore, if you're about to get hitched, especially if you're a woman, here are two issues to ponder before you say, "I do"—snoring and chores.

According to the American Academy of Dental Sleep Medicine, roughly 40 percent of men habitually grunt and rumble in the night compared to 24 percent of women. (An imbalance partly due on biology, as men's larynxes tend to be a tad lower in their necks than women's. Plus compared to women, when men gain weight, they more often distribute fat around their throats that narrows their airways.)[32] While chores-wise in my study, cohabiting-women—compared to their (often male) partners—more often reported doing far more household tasks, such as readying kids for school, despite both parties often working full-time in the labor market.

If we're to restore the nation's pep, there must be action. Suggestions include:

- More of us need to reduce the likelihood of us snoring (from upping our fitness to more of us more frequently replacing our pillows, thereby lowering the amount of allergens in our bedrooms)

- More of us need to divide our chores equally with our partners (from tidying our kids' hair to tidying our toilet bowls), and

- More of us need to practice better "sleep hygiene," which slumber specialist Andrew Hall describes as: "No over-stimulating activities too late at night, [e.g.,] no computers or television, exercising earlier in the day, a little alcohol sometimes, but not too much, and nothing with pilot lights, or bleeping . . . in the bedroom."[33]

But if Americans embraced the common-sense actions above, in an effort to embark on "Operation Goodnight" en masse to restore the nation's restedness, what might happen?[34]

First, sales of miracle products (from astronomically priced face creams to muscle pills) might tumble, because fantastical products appeal less to us when we're brimming with *va va voom*. Second, when Americans stood before their mirrors wondering, "Who's the fairest of us all?" more of them might think, "Me" (i.e., themselves. Not me. Although, thank you for thinking, I'm lovely).

End of Chapter Sidebar: Skincare and the Over 60s

High-end anti-aging skincare seldom targets women aged 60-plus. One reason why is the positivity effect: a cognitive bias that kicks in later in life; wherein, as we age we typically focus more on positive, rather than negative information about ourselves and others. This is appropriate. In old age, we must maintain our immune system, as our biggest enemies tend to be degenerative disease, rather than, for example, backstabbers after our job. The positivity effect also fosters a "Life is short" philosophy that nudges folks to think, "I look good for my age," as opposed to *"Blerg,* look at my deep wrinkles." Having said that, 60-plus-year-olds still want products that nurture and hydrate their skin, but compared to, say, many 35-year-olds, it takes greater effort for 60-plus-year-olds to pretend their $200+ wonder cream is in fact wondrous, because, as a plastic surgeon told me, "Over sixty? Want a miracle? Facelift."[35]

Brain Fuel: If You Study/Work in Advertising

To get a sense of what Photoshop could do for your client's next campaign: 1) visit creativebloq.com, 2) type "100 brilliant print ads" into the search field, 3) pick your favorite ad from the list, and 4) think what the ad made you want to do.

Name a campaign that used Photoshop so poorly the target audience probably felt less inclined to buy the brand after seeing the ads. (Need ideas? Visit psdisasters.com.)

Gather some women's magazines and look at the skincare ads. Note which brands told whoppers and which told white lies. Next, research the prices of these products to establish whether the more expensive ones typically told larger fibs.

High-end skincare ads often overstep advertising's boundary of "permissible exaggeration." Name another category that sells consumers more hype than reality. Next, explain which fantasy that category predominantly sells, e.g., the fantasy of instant attractiveness, power, youth, money, or confidence.

Brain Fuel: If You Study/Work in Marketing

High-end skincare consumers are spoiled for choice. As a result, high-end skincare companies must constantly fathom new ways to foster consumer loyalty, such as offering rewards programs with early access to online sales. Name two other loyalty tactics used by high-end skincare companies.

As referenceforbusiness.com explains, "Product development is the process by which a company does one of two things: 1) creates an entirely new product that either adds to an existing product line or occupies an entirely new niche, and 2) modifies or upgrades an existing product." Imagine you're in charge of product development at a real high-end skincare company, such as La Mer. Once you've selected which company you fancy working at, check out their products on their website. Next, think about how you might alter one of their existing products, e.g., its size, sales description, name, packaging, fragrance, and/or consistency?

If you were to launch a rejuvenating hair product for men, what might you name it? What might its packaging look like? And how might you distribute it, e.g., online, in stores; and if in stores, which stores? (Thought starter for ten: you could name it "Hair Today, Not Gone Tomorrow." That's why I'm not a copywriter.)

Fieldwork for All

Visit a drugstore to observe which skincare brands have clear packaging (i.e., you can see the product inside) and which have "veiled" packaging (you can't see the product inside). As you do so, jot down the price per fl. oz. of some of these products to establish whether the veiled products typically cost more than those that are clear-packaged.

Virgin America's decision to install mood lighting inside its lavatories demonstrated consumer-friendly thinking, as flying is unpleasant enough without having to see your fluorescent-lit reflection wearily looking back at you from the confines of a smelly stall. Name three other companies that make clever use of mood lighting inside their planes, trains, automobiles and/or stores, restaurants, or [insert type of business premises]. P.S. the phrase "clever use of mood lighting" is not synonymous with lighting that literally gets you (ahem) "in the mood" (mile-high club notwithstanding).

Notes

1. Photoshop can be a force for good, e.g., the police use it to age images of missing children. (Jeff Schewe, "The Birth of a Killer Application: Ten Years of Photoshop," *Photo Electronic Imaging*, February, 2000.)

2. Thomas Knoll's quote is from an Adobe press release, "Adobe Photoshop Hits Twenty," February 18, 2010.

3. Humans are not alone in our animosity toward being duped. As biologist Robert Trivers explains in *The Folly of Fools*, "Studies from a range of species—wasps, birds, and monkeys—suggest they often get angry and seek immediate retribution [if they suspect they've been hoodwinked]."

4. In 2013, the global anti-aging market—which covers anti-wrinkle products, hair growth treatments and colorants, breast augmentation surgery, and laser services—was estimated to be worth $122.3 billion. (transparencymarketresearch.com).

5. The American Academy of Dermatology's website is aad.org.

6. For more on La Mer, read Sean Poulter, "The Wrinkle Creams That Only Make Your Cash Vanish," *The Daily Mail*. Dec. 14, 2006

7. In the 1990s, high-end skincare ads often featured multi-product regimes, as back then regimes connoted high status: 1) users needed the money to buy them, 2) time to use them, and 3) space to display them. These days, women want to get on with their day. That's why high-end skincare ads often showcase only one item.

8. If you want to celebrate authentic beauty, remember this: miracle makers typically have little financial incentive to tone down their rhetoric. Plus, their fans are often complicit in the temporary feel-good illusions they provide.

9. Medicine shows hark back to medieval Europe.
    (Ann Anderson, *Snake Oil, Hustlers, and Hambones: The American Medicine Show*.)

10. According to social psychologist Daniel Gilbert, "When people daydream about the future, they tend to imagine themselves achieving and succeeding rather than fumbling or failing." Within fantasies, there is no risk, no fear, and no rejection. Whatever we want—passion, respect, power—we get. But clinging to fantasies can prevent us from striding toward the purposeful lives we crave. (Suggested reading: Cynthia Schupak and Jesse Rosenthal, "Excessive Daydreaming: A Case History and Discussion of Mind Wandering and High Fantasy Proneness," *Consciousness and Cognition*, 2009; 18(1):290–292; Daniel Gilbert, Stumbling on Happiness; Jerome L. Singer, *Daydreaming*; and Eric Klinger, "The Power of Daydreams," *Psychology Today*, 1987; 21(10):36–39.)

11. The protagonists in rags-to-riches stories and gold-digger narratives are typically women. Yet throughout history, there have been dandies—skilled in the art of doing nothing—who've sponged off ladies.

12. Beauty ideals shift in relation to a society's culture, economy, and its medical breakthroughs, e.g., during the reign of Queen Elizabeth the First of England (1558–1603) gentlemen court-iers wore crop pants, stockings, and codpieces (the men's push-up bra) to ingratiate themselves with the Virgin Queen. While in 1980s America, the archetype for male beauty became more Herculean thanks to factors, such as the development of anabolic steroids, and an escalation in Cold War tension between the U.S. and the former U.S.S.R.

13. The American Cancer Society advises citizens to avoid the use of supplements claiming to aid with weight loss, bodybuilding, or sexual performance. That's because supplements in the U.S. don't require proof of effectiveness to be sold alongside proven drugs. Visit cancer.org.

14. Oh, please, let's stop pretending men are purely analytical. Men like dreaming too—just ask the editors of *Sports Illustrated* Swimsuit Edition.

15. When Johnson & Johnson bought Rogaine (a.k.a., Regaine in the U.K.), its marketing improved. But its drugstore shelf-positioning remained problematic; the product was often displayed close to non-sexy everyday drugs like unguents for warts, when it might've fared better nearer to luxury hair-care. (Anastasia Toufexis, "Some Bald Facts about Minoxidil," in *Time.* July 14, 1986.)

16. In the 1990s, scientists confirmed that women and men judge men to be older in proportion to how bald they are, and the amount of gray in their hair. (C. J. Bulpitt, H. L. J. Markowe, and M. J. Shipley, "Why Do Some People Look Older than They Should?" *Journal of Postgraduate Medicine*, 2001; 77(911):578–581.)

17. "How would you tackle facial inequality?" In L.P. Hartley's dystopian novel *Facial Justice*, plastic surgeons, at the behest of the government, used scalpels to transform the "facially over-privileged" into the homely. (Michael Efran, "The Effect of Physical Appearance on the Judgment of Guilt, Interpersonal Attraction, and Severity of Recommended Punishment in a Simulated Jury Task," *Journal of Research in Personality*, 1974; 8:45–54.)

18. Which of these common ad tactics used to promote hair-thickening shampoos is sneakier? 1) Cast a spokesperson with hair of average thickness and give her hair extensions in ads, or 2) cast a spokesperson with incredibly thick hair (thank you, genetics) whom the agency had to trawl the nation to find? (Jeffrey Pfeffer, *Power: Why Some People Have It and Others Don't*; Alex Brownsell, "Cheryl Cole's L'Oréal Ad Escapes ASA Ban," in *Campaign.* June 2, 2010; Andrew Adam Newman, "Mascara Ads: Thick Lashes, Fine Print," in *The New York Times.* Nov. 12, 2013.)

19. In 1838, Charles Darwin, age 29, apparently climbed into a cage at London Zoo to get closer to an orangutan named Jenny who'd been staring at herself in a mirror, as Charles wanted to know: "Did Jenny recognize herself?" His observations were inconclusive. Over 100 years later, psychologist George Gallup Jr. used a version of the rouge test to see whether primates did indeed know their own reflections. His findings: "After prolonged exposure to their reflected images in mirrors, chimpanzees marked with red dye [on their faces] showed evidence of being able to recognize their own reflections [unlike monkeys]." (Charles Darwin and Carl Zimmer, *The Descent of Man: The Concise Edition*; Gordon G. Gallup Jr., "Chimpanzees: Self-Recognition," *Science*, 1970; 167(3914):86–87; Beulah Amsterdam, "Mirror Self-Image Reactions before Age Two," *Developmental Psychology*, 1973; 5(4):297–305.)

20. Robert Franks' quote is from *Luxury Fever*.

21. In their book *Willpower*, Roy F. Baumeister and John Tierney state: "Nature doesn't really care whether you feel good [about yourself]. It selects for traits that improve survival and reproduction." In summary, self-awareness in humans didn't develop to make us happy. As Baumeister and Tierney go on to explain, "Psychologists Charles Carver and Michael Scheier . . . arrived at a vital insight: self-awareness evolved because it helps self-regulation." That's why, when we see our reflections, we often compare ourselves to standards we've set for ourselves.

22. More women than men, in my study, when asked about their recent reflections mentioned wrinkles. Is that because women's faces wrinkle more deeply than men's? Not necessarily. For while a man's skin does typically wrinkle less than a woman's, men typically take less care of their skin. So, why the disparity? Reasons include: 1) a higher percentage of women than men had said they'd looked tired, and tiredness makes us hyper-critical of every aspect of our appearance, and 2) some chaps were likely too focused on their thinning hair to comment

on anything else. (Diana Howard, "Is a Man's Skin Really Different?" dermalinstitute.com.)

23. Out of the four personality types, Explorers most often thought they'd recently looked good in the mirror. This could partly be related to their love of exercise.

24. In my study, more women than men, aged 18–29, criticized their hair in front of the mirror. From age 30 onward, this trend reversed.

25. In the 1920s, Émile Coué's self-help book *Self-Mastery through Conscious Autosuggestion* inspired countless people to chant like sorcerers: "Every day, in every way, I'm getting better and better." But I'm not advocating the use of positive affirmations to improve American's well-being, because psychologists have found that when people with low self-esteem repeat positive affirmations to themselves their moods often worsen, because, for them, the words ring hollow. (Joanne Wood and others, "Positive Self-Statements: Power for Some, Peril for Others," *Psychological Science*, 2009; 20(7):860–866.)

26. Millions of people treat tiredness as a medical problem, when for many it's a lifestyle problem not aided by coffee and sleeping pills. (Roni Caryn Rabin, "New Worries about Sleeping Pills," in *The New York Times*. March 12, 2012.)

27. Some unmarried adults in my study might've looked tired in their mirrors due to their prior playful shenanigans.

28. In the table, "America's Energy Crisis," single moms and dads were absent. Why? My sample size of single dads was teeny, and my sample size of single moms was small. Take this with a pinch of salt, in my study, roughly 60 percent of single moms said they'd recently looked tired in the mirror.

29. Martin Seligman's quote is from *Authentic Happiness*.

30. Daniel Gilbert's quote is from Christopher Munsey, "Does Marriage Make Us Happy?" in apa.org. October 2010.

31. If you're a numbers person, you'll love this. One of my survey questions asked: *"Looking back over the past year, how do you feel about these aspects of your life? Treated people as I would like to be treated; improved my knowledge and skills; eased up on self-criticism; exercised and nourished my body; allowed my inner-child to play; felt supported by family, friends, colleagues, and government; found locations where I could recharge and be myself; felt loved in relationships; and, managed my money efficiently."* Next, my respondents scored each category from 1 to 10, where 1 = dreadful and 10 = perfect (giving a potential maximum score of 90). The average total score for 18- to 44-year-old married or cohabiting Negotiators (with or without kids) was 54.5. For 18- to 44-year-old single Negotiators (with or without kids), it was 50.2. These scores should be treated with caution. Calculating happiness is complex. Also, not all categories in the above question carry the same weight for individuals.

32. The American Academy of Dental Sleep Medicine's website is aadsm.org.

33. Snore much? Visit webmd.com. (Andrew Hall's quote is from Laura Barton, "Sleeping Pills: Britain's Hidden Addiction," in *The Guardian.* Aug. 20, 2012.)

34. If you fancy embarking on "Operation Goodnight," know this: healthy habits take around 66 days to form, rather than the oft-cited 21 days quoted in various ads. (Phillippa Lally and others, "How Are Habits Formed: Modeling Habit Formation in the Real World," *European Journal of Social Psychology,* 2010; 40:998–1009.)

35. For more on the positivity effect, read Stefanie Brassen and others, "Anterior Cingulate Activation is Related to a Positivity Bias and Emotional Stability in Successful Aging," *Biological Psychiatry,* 2011; 70(2):131.

CHAPTER FIVE

Wisdom

"I know one thing, that I know nothing."
—Socrates

Wisdom gets handed down from parent to child, teacher to student, and stranger to stranger. Over 2,000 years ago on the Silk Road, camel-weary merchants traded more than goods; they traded art, music, and belief systems that influenced people's minds, hearts, and religions. In the 1600s, when Newton revolutionized physics, he did so (in his words) by "standing on the shoulders of giants," such as Descartes and Galileo.[1] And in the 1700s, when Jefferson drafted the Declaration of Independence in less than three weeks(!), he peppered in thoughts from ancient Greek, Roman, and Enlightenment philosophers, whose books he'd long and lovingly studied.[2]

But these days, where do Americans get their wisdom? Is it the Bible—that transformative and enduring book—that psychologist Steven Pinker describes as "a wiki . . . . compiled over half a millennium from writers with different styles, [and] dialects"?[3] Or, when Americans feel rudderless, do they consult Pulitzer Prize winners,

People magazine, or the position of Pluto in their horoscopes? (Hello, fellow Librans.)

In addition to all that, this chapter also reveals what folks would do, should they become President of the United States. Me: On my first morning, I'd skydive out of Air Force One onto the White House's lawn in a pantsuit emblazoned with bald-headed eagles. But unfortunately for you, I'm ineligible for office, as I was born in Britain. (What can I say? I'd be ~~awful~~ amazing at the job.)

This Much I Know

One of the best parts of my job is asking folks questions, then—wait for it—listening. I've learned a ton. Motorists have taught me how to pimp my ride. Cruise-ship mavens have taught me where to find love at sea (full disclosure: bars on the lido deck). And *World of Warcraft* players have taught me how to slaughter hordes. But until the study in this book, I'd never asked anyone in America to: *"Share the wisest quote you have heard or read, or share your own piece of wisdom."* And I should've, because the answers reveal:

- What parents have been schooling their kids beyond "Always wear clean underpants," and

- Which beliefs are shaping—and have shaped— America's culture

Cultural data is of use to anyone involved in spin; as biologist Richard Dawkins explains, "Among animals, man is uniquely dominated by culture."[4] It influences our opinions on everything, from the desirability and best age to get married, to which food to serve on Thanksgiving, to whether or not it's appropriate for men to cry in public other than at funerals and at football matches after their favorite team has been trounced.

So roll up and lend an ear to hear the most hallowed wisdom of Americans, which I've assembled into ten handy categories:

Ten Lessons for Successful Living
(in reverse order, a la David Letterman)

10. Be Yourself

Three percent of Americans (six percent on the West Coast) chose *be yourself* for their most important life lesson. This motto encompasses being yourself at work, home, and anyplace in-between. After all, telling a beau you love nightclubbing—when you love not going out— can lead to sweaty misadventures of the techno-blaring kind. While telling a boss you love mornings, when you're among the 16 percent of the population that's genetically predisposed to being a night owl can lead to fatigue, should your boss move you to an earlier shift.[5] Also, when folks hide their sexuality from themselves and others, it threatens their ongoing happiness, because whenever we maintain a façade it limits our ability to identify and value our signature strengths.[6] Useful tangent: advertising slogans aimed at teens, such as Burger King's "Your Way," often contain a *be you* message, as our species' search for identity often hits that age group hardest.[7]

9. Be Curious

Curiosity is the hallmark of scientists, artists, and pioneers driven by the belief that the pursuit of knowledge is the most satisfying way to live. Five percent of Americans chose *be curious* for the life lesson they most heartily endorse. This group's favorite quotes were: "Learn something new every day" and Apple's slogan "Think different" that champions a *be curious* message to sell products to—you've guessed it—scientists, artists, and pioneers.

8. Be Playful

Humor is a psychological coping technique born from adversity. That's why comedians often grow-up in places like Detroit, not Beverly Hills (where hardship can entail your butler serving you lethargically shaken martinis. It's so hard to get good staff these days.)[8] Six percent of my respondents, among whom Midwesterners were overrepresented, selected *be playful* for their top life lesson. Their favorite quotes were "Dance like no one is watching" and "A day without laughter is a day wasted"—the latter attributed to slapstick legend Charlie Chaplin. Real-world application: car-insurance ads often cheekily remind consumers to "Always look on the bright side of life" (cue *Monty Python* song), because drivers buy insurance to get themselves through life's bumps. (Note to self: Stop using British cultural references in this splendid chapter on American culture!)

7. Brown Happens

Our world is predictably unpredictable. Earthquakes, traffic jams, and tsunamis are side effects of living on a planet with wobbly crust and over seven billion people. Enter the life lesson: *shit happens*. That frankest of phrases that reminds us life is often unfair. In my study, the following respondents agreed that in America good things happen to villains and bad things happen to goodies, suggesting Karma's been asleep on the job:

- 85 percent of over-60-year-olds versus
  59 percent of 18–34-year-olds
- 67 percent of Midwesterners versus
  59 percent of the rest of the nation
- 65 percent of atheists versus
  62 percent of believers in God/gods, and
- 64 percent of women versus 57 percent of men

The above findings support psychologist Steven Pinker's assessment that the extent to which an individual believes in *shit happens* is influenced more by his or her's experience than by their religious philosophy.[9]

6. Be Persistent

Newsflash. Forget genius: greatness takes grit. That's the word from scientists who say, "Many characteristics once believed to reflect innate talent are . . . the result of intense practice for a minimum of ten years."[10] Ten years! Hence the allure of spurious shortcuts to success, from ordering diplomas from Nonesuch University dot edu (as opposed to attending a nonfictional university) to swallowing over-the-counter laxatives—talk about *shit happens*! But whatever your goals (closets full of size 6s to cupboards full of trophies), the top lesson of eight percent of Americans was *be persistent*. Their favorite quote? "If at first you don't succeed, try, try again."[11]

5. Be Responsible

In a land with hot-dog-stuffed-crust pizza, you might've expected *be responsible* not to have made this list. (Kidding! Lots of Americans are sensible.) The top quotes among those choosing *be responsible* were: "In the house of the wise are stores of choice food and oil, but a foolish man devours all he has" (Proverbs 21:20 NIV); "Common sense is not so common" (attributed to French philosopher Voltaire); and "Don't eat yellow snow" (*umm*, attributed to Eric Theodore Cartman—I'm guessing).[12] In regard to Voltaire's quote (true story), a chap once misquoted it to a tattooist, and the chap's derriere now reads: "Common sense is not that common," giving new meaning to the term "bottom line." But butt puns aside, humans are often silly, because, despite our magnificent brains:

- Our IQs dip when we feel rejected[13]

- Our urges for food and sex are powerful, and

- Our psychology, biology, and our environment causes our willpower to fluctuate, e.g., at the supermarket, once you've resisted putting beer, burritos, and bourbon ice-cream into your cart, is it any wonder why so many of us say "Yes" to buying candy at the checkout? (Google: "Decision making fatigue")[14]

4. Be Mindful

In any given year, an estimated 20 to 25 percent of U.S. adults have a mental health issue.[15] America is stressed, some places more than others. In my study, respondents from states like Hawaii and

Wyoming, which rank highly in Gallup polls for best places to live, seldom chose *be mindful* for their life lesson, unlike folks in states like California, Texas, and New Jersey. (L.A's gridlock could rankle Buddha. Stop that, Buddha. There's no need to flip the bird.)

The most popular quotes amongst those choosing *be mindful* were 1) "Living one day at a time" from the Serenity Prayer, which gets recited at AA meetings, and 2) phrases along the lines of "You deserve a break today."

Here's a valuable tangent: in the 1970s, McDonald's then-slogan "You deserve a break today" leveraged a psychological phenomenon known as the licensing effect that works like this—whenever we deplete our willpower and energy on chores, our subconscious says, "treat yourself" to ensure we'll:

- Replenish our bodies and minds, and

- Keep doing chores in the future, as the licensing effect strengthens the association in our minds that whenever we finish some chore, we give ourselves a treat

But what to choose? Hunter-gatherers would've picked something relatively healthy, whereas we often opt for soda, candy, or fast food, because they're 1) everywhere, 2) often delicious, 3) relatively inexpensive, and 4) many of us regard them as befitting rewards upon the completion of everyday tasks, as billions of dollars have been spent advertising them as such for over 85 years.[16]

However, when soda, candy, and fast-food companies began supersizing their products, they mucked up this equation. One solution? To re-downsize their products, indicating that even for goods like candy, size matters.[17]

Are we done yet? Three lessons to go!

3. Be All In

Be all in was always going to win a medal in this countdown, as the U.S. doesn't do half-assed. Case in point, the Walmart Superstore at Crossroads Commons, Albany, New York, which, at 260,000 sq. ft., is similar in size to four and a half football fields. That's why it's getting four stars as *the* place to ride out the zombie apocalypse. The top quote among those selecting *be all in* was "Live life to the fullest."

2. Be Hopeful

When a 2014 poll from *NBC* and *The Wall Street Journal* asked Americans, "[Will] life for our children's generation be better than it has been for us?" 76 percent of their respondents thought not.[18] Yet when I asked Americans, *"An independent single woman in her 20s seeks a lifetime of financial gain. Which career strategy should she take up?"* only two percent advised, "Emigration."[19] Because when all's said and done, the U.S. is one of the best countries in the world in which to fulfill your potential (according to United Nations data).[20]

But, no "spoiler alert" needed here, life in the U.S. is not all "Ha ha. Hee hee." Enter the lesson *be hopeful*, chosen by 10 percent of citizens. Their top quotes were (in reverse order):

- "Don't worry, be happy" (attributed to Indian guru Meher Baba and many others)

- "Everything happens for a reason" (not from the Bible, as many assume)

- "This too shall pass" (attributed to medieval Persian poets), and

- "I can do all this through Him who gives me strength" (Philippians 4:13 NIV)

There are reasons to be hopeful in the dark:

- All experiences, great to grisly, enhance our decision-making abilities

- "The whole point of the human brain is behavioral flexibility," explains scholar Robert Wright. In other words, we're wizards at figuring out Plan Bs, when Plan A explodes (Cue *Harry Potter* theme song),[21] and

- The U.S. is home to world-class scientists, doctors, and technologists whose forthcoming breakthroughs may help us in our hour of need (Hey, climate-change scientists, polar bears need polar ice caps. Get on it!)

1. Be Nice

This brings us to the nation's favorite lesson: *be nice*. As well as the nation's favorite quote: "Treat people as you wish to be treated," a.k.a., the golden rule, which pre-dates the advent of Christianity.[22] And while I'm no fan of rules (no surprise there), the golden rule really is golden, because we all prosper when we follow it. For example:

- Common courtesy makes us feel safer among strangers

- An individual's pursuit of happiness relies on others also being happy, and[23]

- Life feels more manageable when we can rely on the kindness and forgiveness of others.[24] Plus, in many industries, niceness gets you bigger tips and larger paychecks making the golden rule a win-win (P.S. No one in my study advocated being a doormat. Nice people often say, "No," too.)

So, now you've heard the Top Ten American Life Lessons, the takeaways are:

1) It's kindness, simple acts of kindness that often make the difference to people's lives[25]

2) (Based on the above) America's moral compass seems to be in excellent hands, as the virtues championed in the lessons—such as love, compassion, courage, responsibility, perseverance, and the pursuit of knowledge—have been at the cornerstone of almost every religious and philosophical tradition for over three thousand years, from Confucianism to the teachings of Plato, and from the Old Testament to the Samurai Code, and[26]

3) Americans get their wisdom from both sources old and new, foreign and domestic

For example, in my study, respondents reached for guidance in the words of Benjamin Franklin, Franklin D. Roosevelt, Thomas Edison, Albert Einstein, Sun Tzu, William Shakespeare, The Rolling Stones,

Bruce Springsteen, Malcolm X, Ralph Waldo Emerson, Muhammad Ali, Victor Hugo, Judge Judy, Gandalf, Yoda, and Nike's world-famous slogan "Just do it" that reminds me of "Have no fear," which appears multiple times in the Bible. Plus, some folks quoted movies, such as *Gladiator*, *Braveheart*, *Star Wars*, *The Shawshank Redemption*, and *Forrest Gump*. (Note to self: For next book, write *The Tao of Tom Hanks*. Chapter One: "My Momma always said, 'Life was like a box of chocolates.'")[27]

Sidebar: The Ads Folks Love to Hate

Before we discover what Americans would do with their wisdom, should they become POTUS, here's a tangent on positive and negative election ads.

Positive political ads seek to convince a cynical electorate that a flesh-and-blood human subject to peccadillo pratfalls (Bill Clinton, anyone?) and public-speaking pratfalls (George W. Bush, anyone?) is qualified to become the (unofficial) leader of the Free World. That's a tough sell. In an attempt to sway voters, positive ads fit into three categories:

- Day-in-the-life ads, in which candidates breakfast with their families before they drive their U.S.-built vehicles to go pat pooches, shake hands, and pucker up to dry-eyed babies

- Outdoorsman/huntress ads, in which candidates hold firearms correctly in the wilderness to demonstrate their skills to be the next Commander-in-Chief, and

- Résumé ads, in which candidates deliver sound bites
  on their five-point policy plans and their just-like-you
  upbringings

But it's negative political ads that devour the lion's share of election media budgets. These fit into two categories:

- Discredit-the-oppositional-candidate ads,
  which seek to nudge citizens who don't support
  the candidate in ads to go out and vote for their
  preferred candidate, and

- Smear-the-oppositional-candidate ads, which ramp
  up the mud-slinging to encourage seldom-voters
  and fence-sitters to abstain from voting altogether,
  because many people, after being carpet-bombed
  with negative political ads, prefer to step aside from
  the ugliness

Who benefits when seldom-voters and fence-sitters don't exercise their right to vote?[28] Often, it's the party with the largest preexisting base.[29]

Hey, Mom, I'm President

Eisenhower said, "Any man who wants to be president is either an egomaniac or crazy." That might explain why, when I asked Americans what they'd do if they were elected to the highest office in the land, 1 percent refused the job—even hypothetically. Because let me ask you this: Would you want to be monitored by the Secret Service all day—trips to the loo included? Or, how about seeing Putin's nipples up close, because we all know how much that man enjoys being shirtless? But Big Brother and Mother Russia aside, here's what the rest of the country said they'd do:

- 0.5 percent said they'd sit back and watch the nation continue its slide into hell

- 1 percent said they'd sit back and let God run the country

- 5 percent said they'd run the country themselves, except they're currently baffled as to ideas (no wonder, complex issues demand complex solutions)[30]

- 17 percent said they'd lead the country toward the goal of everyone *finishing* their lives socially and economically equal[31]

- 35 percent said they'd lead the country toward the goal of everyone being *born* socially and economically equal, and[32]

- 40 percent outlined specific policies, with Republican and Democrat supporters often both stating fairly similar ideas (albeit folks disagreed about funding)

The following quotes all came from Republican supporters (Take note, GOP):[33]

"I would subsidize healthy food and improve working conditions to get people off medications to reduce health care costs."

—44-year-old from Massachusetts

"I would take care of the homeless, the old and veterans. And stop jobs from leaving America."

—67-year-old from Vermont

"I would cleanse the world of corrupt politicians and bankers. And come up with ideas to solve the world's energy problems in an economical and environmental manner."

—63-year-old from Texas

"I would try to see that every child has the opportunity to go to college."

—45-year-old from Jersey

"The rich need to contribute more to those who are trying hard, yet struggling."

—28-year-old from Nevada

Other ideas that waltzed across party lines included:

- Penalize corporate tax evaders

- Accelerate the political apparatus from that of a wheezing tortoise

- Debate wealth inequality without being labeled haters of the superrich, and

- Debate immigration policy

But above all, citizens said that if they were president they'd create opportunity for all, because hope is fine, but it doesn't pay the bills: it's jobs—skillful jobs that pay a decent wage that many Americans believe the nation needs *now*.

Not the American Dream pre-wrapped in a bow to anyone who asks for it, but a chance—a genuine chance—for every woman, man, and child across this country to live their life with dignity and purpose.

Over 125 years ago, Ralph Waldo Emerson wrote, "America is another name for opportunity." His statement: more ambition than fact. Today, many Americans want to know if Emerson's words can be made real. What do you think? Wouldn't it be nice.

Brain Fuel: If You Study/Work in Advertising

Name three ad campaigns for different brands that encourage their respective target audiences to *be yourself*.

Name an industry other than insurance that uses humor in its ads to remind its target audience that *shit happens*.

Various ads have featured versions of the golden rule. For example, "We treat you like you'd treat you" is a tagline used by Discover card. Name another campaign starring the golden rule or something similar.

Type "presidential campaign ads" into YouTube's search field. Then 1) find a positive ad that you think might nudge fence-sitters to vote for the candidate in the ad, and 2) find a negative ad that you think might nudge fence-sitters to abstain for voting.

Brain Fuel: If You Study/Work in Marketing

Name two products/services that empower consumers to embrace the lesson *be curious*.

Name two products/services that empower consumers to embrace the lesson *be all in*.

Name two products/services that empower consumers to embrace the lesson *be nice*.

Think of one of your favorite brands. If you ran product development for that brand, what product might you launch to help your consumers get nearer to fulfilling their American Dream?

Take a moment to think about corporate responsibility and the wishes of American voters. Name a brand that raises funds for schools with the aid of its consumers.

Name a brand that raises funds for the environment with the aid of its consumers.

Name a brand that raises funds for job seekers with the aid of its consumers.

Fieldwork for All

Ask a friend to tell you their favorite piece of wisdom. Next, consider how your friend's behavior reflects their choice, e.g., if they chose the golden rule, how do they regularly display consideration toward others? (In marketing speak, "Are they true to their brand?")

What's your favorite piece of wisdom? Over the next week, try to see whether this piece of wisdom (or something similar to it) crops up in your environment. For example, you might see it on a T-shirt or a magnet, or perhaps you'll hear it in a song, a radio spot, or a movie.

Before the next presidential election, multiple candidates will likely campaign on the platform of "creating opportunity for all." Your task? To ascertain whether these candidates have actionable policy ideas to make opportunity happen.

Notes

1. Newton possibly cribbed the phrase "standing on the shoulders of giants" from 12th-century philosopher Bernard of Chartres. (John of Salisbury and Daniel D. McGarry, *The Metalogicon of John of Salisbury*.)

2. In 1771, Jefferson compiled a reading list for his friend Robert Skipwith. The list included books on Socrates, Plutarch and Seneca, as well as books by Enlightenment philosophers, such as David Hume. Five years after sending the list, Jefferson drafted the Declaration of Independence. (Douglas L. Wilson, "Thomas Jefferson's Library and the Skipwith List," *Harvard Library Bulletin*, 1992; 3(4):56–72; Gary Wills and Thomas Jefferson, *Inventing America: Jefferson's Declaration of Independence*.)

3. Steven Pinker's quote is from *The Better Angels of Our Nature*.

4. Our brains notice behavioral cues from people in our visual field, be they physically present or in the media. These cues influence our actions often toward conformity, especially when we are amidst strangers. For more, Google "Asch conformity experiments." (Richard Dawkins' quote is from *The Selfish Gene*.)

5. Our circadian rhythms are influenced by the PER1 gene that has two main variants: adenine (A) and guanine (G). The first predisposes a person to be an early riser. The second: a late riser. In a recent study, 36% of the population was shown to have the AA genotype; 16%, the GG genotype; and 48%, a combination of A and G. (Andrew S. P. Lim and others, "A Common Polymorphism near PER1 and the Timing of Human Behavioral Rhythms," *Annals of Neurology*, 2012; 72: 324–334.)

6. Oscar Wilde said, "Be yourself; everyone else is already taken," yet in late 19th-century England, when his private life became public, he was sentenced to two years' hard labor. Had he been sentenced in the U.S., the result would've also been harrowing,

e.g., in Virginia in that era, the minimum penalty for sex between consenting men was two years' imprisonment with a five-year maximum. Previously it had been a death penalty offense. (Jack Drescher, "The Closet: Psychological Issues of Being In and Coming Out," in *Psychiatric Times*. Oct. 1, 2004; Richard Ellman, *Oscar Wilde*; and, *A Collection of All Acts of the General Assembly of Virginia*, 1802.)

7. Burger King's slogan "Your Way" combines its selling proposition (there are more ways to customize a Whopper than a Big Mac) with our species' search for identity.

8. Humor is most effective as a coping strategy when we like the prankster and believe the prankster's type of humor fits the situation. (Charles R. Gruner, "Wit and Humor in Mass Communication," in A. J. Chapman and H. C. Foot (eds.), *Humor and Laughter: Theory, Research and Applications*.)

9. George Bernard Shaw wrote in his play *Major Barbara*, "People may differ about matters of opinion, or even about religion; but how can they differ about right and wrong? Right is right; and wrong is wrong; and if a man cannot distinguish them properly, he is either a fool or a rascal." In my study, atheists and those with religious beliefs valued the same life lessons. (Steven Pinker discusses "shit happens" in *The Better Angels of Our Nature*.)

10. For more on the power of grit, read K. Anders Ericsson, Ralf Krampe, and Clemens Tesch-Römer, "The Role of Deliberate Practice in the Acquisition of Expert Performance," *Psychological Review*, 1993; 3:363–406.

11. The popularity of the proverb "If at first you don't succeed, try, try again" often rises during wartime and stressful peacetime, albeit the words change. For example, in the run-up to the Second World War, the British government produced millions of "Keep calm and carry on" posters to be distributed across the country in the event of a national catastrophe, such as if

German troops had invaded British soil. (Stuart Hughes, "The Greatest Motivational Poster Ever?" in bbc.co.uk. Feb 4, 2009.)

12. Mr. Cartman appears on the television show *South Park*.

13. What happens when we get dumped? Read Guy Winch, "Ten Surprising Facts about Rejection," in *Psychology Today*. July 3, 2013

14. Next time you're at the supermarket, shop back-to-front (start at the frozen foods and end at the produce) to see whether you wind up with a "healthier" cart.

15. U.S. mental health statistics are available at nimh.nih.gov.

16. One of Coca-Cola's retired slogans from the 1920s was "The Pause That Refreshes." Kit Kat's current U.S. slogan is "Break Time. Anytime."

17. Corporations fib about food; so do we. When people join gyms, many gain weight because folks like to pretend their workouts justify decadent post-exercise snacking. (John Tierney and Roy Baumeister, *Willpower*.)

18. A 2001 poll from *The Wall Street Journal* and *NBC* asked, "[Will] life for our children's generation be better than it has been for us," 43 percent of the poll's respondents thought not. (Dana Milbank, "Americans' Optimism is Dying," in *The Washington Post*. Aug. 12, 2014.)

19. In my study, the top-answer to the question *"An independent single woman in her 20s seeks a lifetime of financial gain. Which career strategy should she take up?"* was *"Hard work, determination and avoidance of debt."*

20. According to the U.N.'s *Human Development Index* (using 2013 data), the best country to develop your potential in is Norway. Fifth best? The U.S.A. (hdr.undp.org).

21. Robert Wright's quote is from *The Moral Animal*.

22. In my study, roughly 14 percent of women and 14 percent of men chose the golden rule for their wisest quote. The biblical passage that refers to the preexisting golden rule reads, "So in everything, do to others what you would have them do to you, for this sums up the Law and the Prophets" (Matthew 7:12 NIV).

23. Witnessing rudeness toward others impairs our concentration and well-being. Once we exit the toxic situation, our mood often bounces back. (Rebecca A. Clay, "That's Just Rude," *Monitor on Psychology*, 2013; 44(10):34; Kaja Perina, "Misery Loves Company," in *Psychology Today*, October 13, 2006.)

24. In *The Way We Never Were*, historian Stephanie Coontz explains: ". . . Research in social history demonstrates that early American families were dependent upon a large network of neighbors, church institutions, courts, government officials, and legislative bodies for their sustenance." In other words, Americans have always relied on the kindness of others despite the nation's ethos of American individualism.

25. Many Americans think the nation's getting ruder. But present-day behavior is not that bad considering past events, e.g., I'll take "manspreaders" on subways any day over witch burnings. For more, read Norbert Elias, *The Civilizing Process*. (For polls on perceived U.S. incivility, go to rasmussenreports.com.)

26. According to Katherine Dahlsgaard and her colleagues, the following virtues have remained popular throughout history: love and humanity, spirituality and transcendence, the advancement of knowledge, temperance, justice, and courage. Together, these virtues fortify friendships and trade. Tangent: The virtues favored by a society are influenced by factors including: its economy, medical know-how, the desires of its dominant class, and how the middle class thinks it can best gain status, e.g., in Victorian times, when an estimated 5 to 20 percent of Europeans and Americans had or would get

syphilis, "chastity" was championed among Western countries. (Katherine Dahlsgaard, Christopher Peterson, and Martin E. P. Seligman, "Shared Virtue: The Convergence of Valued Human Strengths across Culture and History," *Review of General Psychology*, 2005; 9(3):203–213; Robert Kaplan, "Syphilis, Sex and Psychiatry, 1789-1925: Part 2," *Australasian Psychiatry*, 2010; 18(1):22–27.)

27. This chapter focused on life lessons given by the majority of my respondents. But roughly 10 percent of my respondents gave examples of subculture wisdom, such as "Do unto others before they f*ck you," "Sometimes being a bitch is all you have to hold on to," and "The scariest words in English are 'We are from the government and we are here to help.'"

28. Less than 60 percent of eligible citizens voted in the 2012 presidential election despite unprecedented spending on political ads. These ads were overwhelmingly negative, so, in one sense, they did their job. Other reasons for the turnout included the inconvenience of voting, and the widespread belief among citizens that they wield little power in political affairs. When I asked folks: *"During the past year, who has wielded the most power over Americans' daily lives?"* their top answers were 1) bankers, 2) corporations, 3) oil tycoons, 4) big pharma, and 5) politicians—who fundraise from the previous groups. Only two percent said, "Voters." However, as political scientist Eric Oliver explains, low voter turnout can reflect *high* voter contentment, as political participation has been seen to decline in areas that are both high in social homogeneity and low in social conflict. As such, citizens who abstain from voting to show their disgust with modern politics risk having their actions misconstrued. (J. Eric Oliver, *Democracy in Suburbia*; Martin Gilens and Benjamin I. Page, "Testing Theories of American Politics: Elites, Interest Groups and Average Citizens," *Perspectives on Politics*, 2014; 12(3):562–581; and Ezra Klein, "The Most Depressing Graphic for Members of Congress," in *The Washington Post.* Jan. 14, 2013.)

29. Candidates should avoid running solely negative campaigns, because their predicted voters need to see them being nice— if only on occasion. (Daniel Kahneman, Paul Slovic and Amos Tversky (eds.), *Judgment Under Uncertainty: Heuristics and Biases*.)

30. At the 1788 Virginia Ratifying Convention soon-to-be-President James Madison said, "The people will have the virtue and intelligence to select men of virtue and wisdom [to govern the nation]." But for voters to make informed decisions, skilled journalists are needed to deconstruct referenda issues for us.

31. Citizens who said they'd lead the country to the place where everyone *finishes* life socially and economically equal often identified themselves as having the Negotiator personality type whose happiness is acutely affected by the well-being of others.

32. Citizens who said they'd lead the country toward one where folks are *born* socially and economically equal often identified their personality type as being the Builder whose happiness is tied to living in harmonious neighborhoods.

33. In my study, 26 percent of respondents who said they favored the Republicans' economic policies also said they favored the Democrats' social policies. The reverse was less pronounced: among those who favored the Democrats' economic policies, only 11 percent said they favored the Republicans' social policies. Even among Conservative Republicans, 13 percent said they favored the Democrats' social policies. (Jaime Fuller, "Voters Like Democrats Better than Republicans on Virtually Every Issue. But That Doesn't Mean They Will Vote for Them," in *The Washington Post*. May 1, 2014.)

CHAPTER SIX

The Dubious Science of the Social Sciences

"There are three kinds of lies: lies, damned lies, and statistics."

—Benjamin Disraeli

Our world is awash in statistics: sports statistics, education statistics, climate-change statistics, vital statistics. You name it, some folks just love getting all up in their data. But as you know, some statistics are purposefully misleading, especially those collected and analyzed by organizations benefitting from the results. (If drug cartels published studies on cocaine, the findings might read: "No side effects. Cocaine's great.") So, is the data in this book reliable? *You* decide in this chapter. But before we get into how my study was carried out, let's talk "researcher bias."

One of the first textbooks I was instructed to read as a sociology undergraduate was Émile Durkheim's *The Rules of Sociological Method*, in which Durkheim wrote, "Our main goal [as sociologists] is to extend scientific rationalism to human conduct." In plain English, sociologists (and other social scientists) should attempt to analyze and quantify human emotions and behavior with the rigor of "hard" scientists, e.g., physicists, chemists, and biologists. But unlike the topics studied by folks in white lab coats (Clinique salespersons don't count!), the topics I study defy mathematical precision. That's why conclusions in the social sciences are *heavily* tainted by how researchers interpret their data. Consequently, I strive to be impartial, but the findings in this book have been shaped by my beliefs. These include:

- Social scientists (which includes account planners) should study what unites us, not only what divides us, because to paraphrase John Steinbeck, "In every bit of honest [research] . . . there is a base theme. Try to understand [people]; if you understand each other you will be kind to each other." I, too, want to live in a world where we feel more connected and less suspicious of one another

- Humans can be foolish, but we're also savvy. Whenever I interview someone, they teach me a ton, irrespective of their income, qualifications, or professions

- Life is tough. I'm constantly amazed by the perseverance of folks who, as worries crowd their minds, keep going to work and putting food on the table, when there are so many other options, like screaming in the street or retreating under a duvet with a box of wine, and

- Humans have a dark side. As psychologist Steven Pinker explains, ". . . Most of us—including you, dear reader—are wired for violence, even if in all likelihood we will never have an occasion to use it."[1] Fortunately, for our species, our innate desire to scratch and spit typically declines after the hotheaded age of two[2]

Methodology

A couple of years ago, I had a madcap idea to conduct a study. Its grand title? "The American Meaning of Life Project." It was one of those nights when one toys with the notion of becoming a 21st-century Alexis de Tocqueville. (If you didn't think I was odd before, you will now. Oh, and if the name de Tocqueville didn't ring a bell, he was the Frenchman who toured the United States in the 1800s to learn more of "its character, its prejudices, and its passions," before writing *Democracy in America: Volumes 1 and 2*.)

When this idea struck, I'd been feeling stuck. In that, I'd been living in Los Angeles for a decade. And while I felt the research I'd been conducting for clients in my role as head of account planning gave more insight into the human condition than sayings inside fortune-cookies, I'd grown concerned that my perspective on life was now too Southern California-centric. Let's face it, Los Angeles is odd, especially the Westside: a not-so-mystical place near the city's beaches, where ad-agencies often co-exist close to clinics where residents *pay* to get fat sucked out of their thighs and re-injected back into their buttocks. (Neighborhood gentrification in Los Angeles has gotten way out of hand.)

Therefore, it was to broaden my view that I wanted to be Alexis de Tocqueville, rather than Alexis Morell Carrington Colby Dexter Rowan from TV's *Dynasty*. My quest? 1) To explore more of the nation, 2) write surveys based on questions arising on my trip, such as "Truck nuts! What were you thinking, America?" 3) have Americans answer my questions, 4) wallow in glorious data, and, 5) return to my advertising community, a far more useful Brain Sucker.

But before I bade everyone farewell, I wrote a mission statement (Yes, I'm an account planner. It's what we do). This is what I wrote:

The American Meaning of Life Project is an ongoing nationwide study that gathers information on the desires and opinions of U.S. citizens. As such, it seeks to answer:

- *How Americans find fulfillment*

- *How social norms are evolving, and*

- *How American society might be improved for the benefit of all, while allowing individualism to flourish*

While it will also:

- *Explore the foundations of American belief systems*

- *Challenge stereotypes, and*

- *Compare the views of "we the people" to those of established scientists and social scientists*

And that's how I wound up driving West-to-East across the country until I lingered in Charlottesville, Virginia, because it seemed apt to contemplate Americans in Thomas Jefferson's former backyard. There, in the shadow of the Blue Ridge Mountains, I wrote the surveys "Seize the Day" and "Show Me the Money," which formed the foundation to this book. (The question guides to these surveys are available in the appendices.) So now you know the "why," here's the "how."

Distribution

Nationwide survey data often suffers from having non-representative samples. For example, many such surveys overrepresent the views of women and individuals over the age of 60, as those two groups commonly answer a disproportionate amount of surveys compared to the rest of the population. That's not to say that such data isn't useful or fascinating, it likely is. It's just not necessarily valid to call it "nationwide."

How does my study differ? Well, I didn't distribute "Seize the Day" and "Show Me the Money" myself. If I had, I might've been tempted to email a link to the surveys to my advertising friends, resulting in a sample bloated with entertainingly facial-haired, tattooed hipsters.

That's why I contracted market research company Persuadable Research to distribute the surveys and collect the anonymous responses on my behalf. This they did in November 2011, resulting in two samples, each comprised of 2,500 U.S. citizens aged 18 or older (totaling 5,000 complete surveys). Both samples also proportionately matched the U.S. census on:

- Ratio of women to men in America, and

- Ratio of residents in the Northeast, South, West, and Midwest

While each sample closely matched the census on:

- Age distribution (30-plus-year-olds were slightly overrepresented)

- Ratio of Republican supporters to Democratic supporters

- Ratio of atheists to those with religious beliefs, and

- Ratio of U.S. citizens by birth compared to those who were naturalized

As with all surveys, important groups were neglected or under-represented. I apologize. (Yes, I'm British. We say "sorry" a lot.) These groups included:

- People without access to the Internet (because Persuadable Research recruited respondents by way of pop-up ads on websites that, once clicked, redirected individuals to one of the two surveys)

- American ex-pats (the geo-targeted recruitment ads were only visible to those inside the U.S.)

- Folks who never answer surveys (this often includes the über rich), and

- People who write in languages other than English (because I was the one who'd written and would be analyzing the surveys, and my pathetic non-English language skills extend to rude words in French. *Zut alors!*)

Therefore, if you're a researcher, this study is regarded as statistically significant at a confidence level of 0.95 (fabulous for the social sciences, frightful for the hard sciences). And if you're not a researcher, all that means is that percentage differences of 2 percent between groups in this study should not lead to a drama that leads to a crisis—such differences are *well* within its margin of error.

Question Design

Survey writing is an art. And while "Seize the Day" and "Show Me the Money" aren't perfect (Hindsight, I hate you!), I wanted to share some of the thinking that went into their design to inspire you to write your own surveys:

> **Tone of voice.** Survey questions are often written without warmth or charm, in an effort not to unduly influence the mood of respondents. But such questions do influence people; namely, they *bore* them. And I needed folks to feel creative as they described, say, their perfect day. That's why these surveys contain techniques from narrative psychology that invite the swapping of confidences.[3] (Now the words "swapping of confidences" have left my keyboard, I reckon it would be a crackin' title for a period-drama starring Keira Knightley and Anne Hathaway.)

> **Don't dumb it down.** When designing survey questions, it's wise to avoid using words known only to Scrabble champions. That doesn't mean your questions should read like *Dick and Jane*. Patronize your audience and you risk alienating them. Give them intriguing

questions written for adults and you'll be rewarded with wonderful thinking.

Race. Convention dictates surveys must include questions on race/ethnicity. I omitted such questions in this study because race relations in America were beyond the scope of this book. Also, when I trained as a sociologist, I specialized in class, not race—the topic is outside of my area of expertise.

Relationships. In surveys, the oft-used relationship question, "Are you married, single, or divorced/separated/ widowed?" lumps co-habiting individuals in stable (unmarried) relationships into the "single" category. That's silly. That's why, when I write surveys, I often update demographic questions to reflect how people live now, not some stereotype from *The Scarlet Letter*.

And:

Time. Open-ended questions allow respondents to type their opinions into a blank space, rather than forcing them to choose an option from a drop-down menu. The analysis is painstaking—the data, worth it. In this study, Persuadable Research emailed me the raw data files in Excel that I transferred into FileMaker Pro (a database software program with functions like keyword search). Even then, when it came to my open-ended questions, I still read every answer slowly, several times before I began looking for trends.

So, full disclosure: do survey answers precisely represent the views and lives of the people answering them?

No.

At best, survey data provides a hazy snapshot of what respondents had been thinking at the time they read and responded to the questions.[4] At worst, they represent editorialized or fabricated politically correct answers given by folks who disliked the idea of their actual thoughts and deeds being read—and judged—by those coding their answers. For example, the question, "How often did you attend church last month?" is notorious for prompting absentee church-goers to exaggerate their recent attendance. While the question, "Tell me something sensual that you did last night?"—that's engineered to coax gossip—might prompt someone who'd been home alone (except for a sexy bag of Cheetos) to plagiarize lines from *Fifty Shades of Grey*.

But even when people fib on surveys, their answers reveal a mass of information about their nation's culture, its social norms, and how they think they should be living their lives—even if their recent conduct has fallen short of the standards they'd set for themselves. Such data is brilliant; it helps agencies come up with new ways to sell to consumers. More than that, it helps "we the people" come up with new ways to tackle society's needs and wants that—when acted on—might help us live better, together. That, dear reader, is a beautiful thing.[5]

Notes

1. Steven Pinker's quote is from *The Better Angels of Our Nature*.

2. For more on violent children, read David Dobbs, "Terrible Twos Who Stay Terrible," *The New York Times*, December 16, 2013.

3. If you fancy incorporating narrative-psychology techniques into your surveys, read Michael White and David Epston, *Narrative Means to Therapeutic Ends*.

4. Our biology, psychology, and our environment influences how we answer questions, e.g., when researchers at Columbia and Ben-Gurion Universities analyzed 1,000 parole decisions made by judges in the Israeli justice system, they found that prisoners who met with judges just before lunch had a 20 percent chance of appeal, whereas those meeting judges just after lunch had a 60 percent chance of appeal. As the philosopher Montaigne said, "I feel quite a different person before and after lunch. This truism appears in ads for Snickers. (Shai Danziger and others, "Extraneous Factors in Judicial Decisions," *Proceedings of the National Academy of Sciences of the United States of America*, 2011; 108(17): 6889-6892.)

5. I hope you've enjoyed the endnotes. I wanted to gift you with this: in *Man's Search for Meaning*, psychotherapist Viktor Frankl wrote, "Life ultimately means taking the responsibility to find the right answer to its problems and to fulfill the tasks which it constantly sets for each individual. These tasks, and therefore the meaning of life, differ from man to man, and from moment to moment." Good luck finding your answers.

Suggested Reading and References

Adams, Douglas. *The Hitchhiker's Guide to the Galaxy*.
New York: Harmony Books, 1980.

Anderson, Ann. *Snake Oil, Hustlers, and Hambones:
The American Medicine Show*. Jefferson: McFarland
& Company, 2000.

Arendt, Hannah. *The Human Condition*. Chicago:
University of Chicago Press, 1958.

Argyle, Michael. *The Psychology of Happiness*.
London: Methuen, 1987.

Ariely, Dan. *Predictably Irrational: The Hidden Forces That
Shape Our Decisions*. New York: HarperCollins, 2008.

Ariely, Dan. *The Upside of Irrationality: The Unexpected
Benefits of Defying Logic at Work and at Home*.
New York: Harper, 2010.

Axelrod, Robert M. *The Evolution of Cooperation*. Rev. ed.
New York: Basic Books, 2006.

Baron, Jonathan. *Thinking and Deciding*.
New York: Cambridge University Press, 1988.

Barthes, Roland, and Annette Lavers. *Mythologies*.
New York: Hill and Wang, 1972.

Baudrillard, Jean. *The Uncollected Baudrillard*.
Edited by Gary Genosko. London: SAGE, 2001.

Baumeister, Roy F., and John Tierney. *Willpower:
Rediscovering the Greatest Human Strength*.
New York: Penguin Press, 2011.

Bellah, Robert N. *Habits of the Heart: Individualism and
Commitment in American Life*. Berkeley: University
of California Press, 1985.

Berger, Peter L., and Thomas Luckmann. *The Social Construction of Reality: A Treatise in the Sociology of Knowledge*. Garden City: Doubleday, 1966.

de Botton, Alain. *The Consolations of Philosophy*. New York: Pantheon Books, 2000.

Bourdieu, Pierre. *Distinction: A Social Critique of the Judgment of Taste*. Cambridge: Harvard University Press, 1984.

Bryson, Bill. *A Short History of Nearly Everything*. New York: Broadway Books, 2003.

Cappelli, Peter. *The New Deal at Work: Managing the Market-Driven Workforce*. Boston: Harvard Business School, 1999.

Carnegie, Dale. *How to Win Friends and Influence People*. Rev. ed. New York: Simon and Schuster, 1981.

Carroll, Robert Todd. T*he Skeptic's Dictionary: A Collection of Strange Beliefs, Amusing Deceptions, and Dangerous Delusions*. Hoboken: Wiley, 2003.

Carver, Charles S., and Michael Scheier. *On the Self-Regulation of Behavior*. Cambridge: Cambridge University Press, 1998.

Chapman, Antony J., and Hugh Foot, eds. *Humor and Laughter: Theory, Research, and Applications*. London: Wiley, 1976.

Cialdini, Robert B. *Influence: The Psychology of Persuasion*. Rev. ed. New York: Collins, 2007.

Coontz, Stephanie. *The Way We Never Were: American Families and the Nostalgia Trap*. New York: Basic Books, 1992.

Coontz, Stephanie. *Marriage, a History: From Obedience to Intimacy or How Love Conquered Marriage*. New York: Viking, 2005.

Coué, Émile. *Self-Mastery through Conscious Auto-Suggestion*. London: Allen & Unwin, 1959.

Csikszentmihalyi, Mihaly. *Flow: The Psychology of Optimal Experience*. New York: Harper & Row, 1990.

Darwin, Charles. *The Descent of Man*. Princeton: Princeton University Press, 1981.

Dawkins, Richard. *The Selfish Gene*. New ed. Oxford: Oxford University Press, 1989.

Dawkins, Richard. *Unweaving the Rainbow: Science, Delusion, and the Appetite for Wonder*. Boston: Houghton Mifflin, 1998.

Dawkins, Richard. *The God Delusion*. Boston: Houghton Mifflin, 2006.

Dawkins, Richard, and Dave McKean. *The Magic of Reality: How We Know What's Really True*. New York: Free Press, 2011.

Day, Barry, ed. *100 Great Advertisements*. London: Times Newspapers, Mirror Group Newspapers, Campaign Magazine, 1978.

Diamond, Jared M. *Guns, Germs, and Steel: The Fates of Human Societies*. New York: W.W. Norton, 1998.

Diamond, Jared M. *Collapse: How Societies Choose to Fail or Succeed*. New York: Viking, 2005.

Durkheim, E. *Suicide, a Study in Sociology*. Glencoe, Ill.: Free Press, 1951.

Durkheim, E. *The Elementary Forms of the Religious Life*. New York: Free Press, 1965.

Durkheim, E. *The Rules of Sociological Method*. Edited by Steven Lukes. New York: Free Press, 1982.

Ekman, Paul, and Wallace V. Friesen. *Unmasking the Face: A Guide to Recognizing Emotions from Facial Clues*. Englewood Cliffs, N.J.: Prentice-Hall, 1975.

Elias, Norbert. *The Civilizing Process*. New York: Urizen Books, 1978.

Ellmann, Richard. *Oscar Wilde*. Markham: Viking, 1987.

Fischer, David Hackett. *Albion's Seed: Four British Folkways in America*. New York: Oxford University Press, 1989.

Fisher, Helen E. *Why We Love: The Nature and Chemistry of Romantic Love*. New York: H. Holt, 2004.

Fisher, Helen E. *Why Him? Why Her? Finding Real Love by Understanding Your Personality Type*. New York: H. Holt, 2009.

Foucault, Michel. *Madness and Civilization: A History of Insanity in the Age of Reason*. New York: Pantheon Books, 1965.

Frank, Robert H. *Luxury Fever: Weighing the Cost of Excess*. Princeton: Princeton University Press, 2010.

Frankfurt, Harry G. *On Bullshit*. Princeton: Princeton University Press, 2005.

Frankl, Viktor Emil. *Man's Search for Meaning: An Introduction to Logotherapy*. New York: Houghton, Mifflin, 2000.

Freud, Sigmund. *Civilization and Its Discontents*. New York: Cape & Smith, 1930.

Friedan, Betty. *The Feminine Mystique*. New York: W.W. Norton, 1963.

Gatto, John Taylor. *Dumbing Us Down: The Hidden Curriculum of Compulsory Schooling*. Philadelphia: New Society Publishers, 1992.

Gilbert, Daniel Todd. *Stumbling on Happiness*. New York: A.A. Knopf, 2006.

Gladwell, Malcolm. *What the Dog Saw and Other Adventures*. New York: Little, Brown and Company, 2009.

Glover, Jonathan. *Humanity: A Moral History of the Twentieth Century*. New Haven: Yale University Press, 2000.

Goethe, Johann Wolfgang Von, and David Luke. *Faust*. Oxford: Oxford University Press, 1987.

Goffman, Erving. *The Presentation of Self in Everyday Life*. Garden City: Doubleday, 1959.

Goldacre, Ben. *Bad Science*. London: Fourth Estate, 2009.

Graaf, John, and David Wann. *Affluenza: How Overconsumption Is Killing Us and How to Fight Back*. 3rd ed. San Francisco: Berrett-Koehler Publishers, 2014.

Greene, Robert. *The 48 Laws of Power*. New York: Penguin Books, 2000.

Hallowell, Edward M. *Crazy Busy: Overstretched, Overbooked and About to Snap; Strategies for Coping in a World Gone ADD*. New York: Ballantine Books, 2006.

Hammond, Claudia. *Time Warped: Unlocking the Mysteries of Time Perception*. Edinburgh: Canongate Books, 2012.

Hill, Napoleon. *Think and Grow Rich*. 1937 ed. S.I.: Duke Classics, 2012.

Hobbes, Thomas, and J. C. A. Gaskin. *Leviathan*. Oxford: Oxford University Press, 1998.

Hochschild, Arlie Russell. *The Managed Heart: Commercialization of Human Feeling*. Berkeley: University of California, 1983.

Jacobs, Jane. *The Death and Life of Great American Cities*. New York: Vintage, 1992.

James, Oliver. *Office Politics*. London: Vermilion, 2013.

Jefferson, Thomas, and Merrill D. Peterson. *The Portable Thomas Jefferson*. New York: Viking Press, 1975.

John of Salisbury, and Daniel D. McGarry. *The Metalogicon of John of Salisbury*. Berkeley: Calif. University of California Press, 1962.

Jowett, Benjamin. *The Dialogues of Plato*. New York: Random House, 1937.

Kahneman, Daniel, Paul Slovic, and Amos Tversky, eds. *Judgment Under Uncertainty: Heuristics and Biases*. Cambridge: Cambridge University Press, 1982.

Kahneman, Daniel, Ed Diener, and Norbert Schwarz, eds. *Well-being: The Foundations of Hedonic Psychology*. New York: Russell Sage Foundation, 1999.

Keirsey, David, and Marilyn M. Bates. *Please Understand Me II: Temperament, Character, Intelligence*. Del Mar, CA: Prometheus Nemesis, 1998.

Kinder, Donald R., and Cindy D. Kam. *Us against Them: Ethnocentric Foundations of American Opinion*. Chicago: University of Chicago Press, 2009.

Lasch, Christopher. *The Culture of Narcissism: American Life in an Age of Diminishing Expectations*. New York: Norton, 1978.

Lustig, Robert H. *Fat Chance: The Bitter Truth about Sugar*. London: Fourth Estate, 2013.

Maslow, Abraham H. *Toward a Psychology of Being*. 2nd ed. New York: Van Nostrand, 1968.

Medawar, P. B. *Plato's Republic: Incorporating the Art of the Soluble and Induction and Intuition in Scientific Thought*. Oxford: Oxford University Press, 1982.

Merton, Robert King. *Social Theory and Social Structure*. New York: Free Press, 1968.

Miller, Geoffrey F. *The Mating Mind: How Sexual Choice Shaped the Evolution of Human Nature*. New York: Doubleday, 2000.

Nagel, Thomas. *Mortal Questions*. Cambridge: Cambridge University Press, 1979.

Ogilvy, David. *Confessions of an Advertising Man*. New York: Atheneum, 1963.

Ogilvy, David. *Ogilvy on Advertising*. New York: Crown, 1983.

Oliver, J. Eric. *Democracy in Suburbia*. Princeton: Princeton University Press, 2001.

Packard, Vance. *The Hidden Persuaders*. New York: D. McKay, 1957.

Peale, Norman Vincent. *The Power of Positive Thinking.* New York: Prentice-Hall, 1952.

Pfeffer, Jeffrey. *What Were They Thinking? Unconventional Wisdom about Management.* Boston: Harvard Business School Press, 2007.

Pfeffer, Jeffrey. *Power: Why Some People Have It and Others Don't.* New York, NY: HarperBusiness, 2010.

Pink, Daniel H. *A Whole New Mind: Why Right-Brainers Will Rule the Future.* New York: Riverhead Books, 2006.

Pink, Daniel H. *Drive: The Surprising Truth about What Motivates Us.* New York: Riverhead Books, 2009.

Pinker, Steven. *Words and Rules: The Ingredients of Language.* New York: Basic Books, 1999.

Pinker, Steven. *The Better Angels of Our Nature: Why Violence Has Declined.* New York: Viking, 2011.

Putnam, Robert D. *Bowling Alone: The Collapse and Revival of American Community.* New York: Simon & Schuster, 2000.

Riesman, David, and Nathan Glazer. *The Lonely Crowd: A Study of the Changing American Character.* Abridged and Rev. ed. New Haven: Yale University Press, 2001.

Sagan, Carl. *The Dragons of Eden: Speculations on the Evolution of Human Intelligence.* New York: Random House, 1977.

Seligman, Martin E. P. *Helplessness: On Depression, Development, and Death.* San Francisco: W.H. Freeman, 1975.

Seligman, Martin E. P. *Authentic Happiness: Using the New Positive Psychology to Realize Your Potential for Lasting Fulfillment.* New York: Free Press, 2002.

Simonton, Deborah. *A History of European Women's Work: 1700 to the Present.* London: Routledge, 1998.

Singer, J. L. *Daydreaming: An Introduction to the Experimental Study of Inner Experiences*. New York: Random House, 1966.

Singer, Peter. *The Expanding Circle: Ethics and Sociobiology*. New York: Farrar, Straus & Giroux, 1981.

Smiles, Samuel. *Self-Help: With Illustrations of Conduct and Perseverance*. Centenary ed. London: J. Murray, 1958.

Steel, Jon. *Truth, Lies, and Advertising: The Art of Account Planning*. New York: Wiley, 1998.

Thaler, Richard H., and Cass R. Sunstein. *Nudge: Improving Decisions about Health, Wealth, and Happiness*. New Haven: Yale University Press, 2008.

Thomas, Lewis. *The Fragile Species*. New York: Scribner's, 1992.

Thorne, Barrie. *Rethinking the Family: Some Feminist Questions*. New York: Longman, 1982.

de Tocqueville, Alexis. *Democracy in America (complete)*. Cirencester: Echo Library, 2005.

Trivers, Robert. *The Folly of Fools: The Logic of Deceit and Self-Deception in Human Life*. New York: Basic Books, 2011.

Underhill, Paco. *Why We Buy: The Science of Shopping*. New York: Simon & Schuster, 1999.

Underhill, Paco. *What Women Want: The Global Marketplace Turns Female Friendly*. New York: Simon & Schuster, 2010.

Veblen, Thorstein. *The Theory of the Leisure Class; an Economic Study of Institutions*. New York: Macmillan, 1899.

Weber, Max. *The Protestant Ethic and the Spirit of Capitalism*. Student's ed. New York: Scribner, 1958.

Weiland, Matt, and Sean Wilsey, eds. *State by State: A Panoramic Portrait of America*. New York: Ecco, 2008.

White, Michael, and David Epston. *Narrative Means to Therapeutic Ends*. New York: Norton, 1990.

Whyte, William Hollingsworth. *The Essential William H. Whyte*. Edited by Albert LaFarge. New York: Fordham University Press, 2000.

Wills, Garry, and Thomas Jefferson. *Inventing America: Jefferson's Declaration of Independence*. London: Athlone, 1980.

Wing, R. L. *The Art of Strategy: A New Translation of Sun Tzu's Classic, The Art of War*. New York: Doubleday, 1988.

Wolf, Naomi. *The Beauty Myth: How Images of Beauty Are Used against Women*. New York: W. Morrow, 1991.

Wright, Robert. *The Moral Animal: The New Science of Evolutionary Psychology*. New York: Pantheon Books, 1994.

Wuthnow, Robert. *Acts of Compassion: Caring for Others and Helping Ourselves*. Princeton: Princeton University Press, 1991.

"Seize the Day" Question Guide

Is today turning out as you expected?

Or is someone else calling the shots?
In this survey, you'll ponder perfect days and the importance of power.

(The following question guide features skip logic and coding instructions unseen by respondents.)

1. In which of the following youthful age ranges does your age fall?

Under 18 *(Exit survey)*	40–44	65–69
18–24	45–49	70–74
25–29	50–54	75–79
30–34	55–59	80+
35–39	60–64	

2. In which fabulous year were you born?

   19___

3. Are you a U.S. citizen, age 18 and over?

   Yes   No *(Exit survey)*

4. In which country was your little body born?

   USA *(Skip to 6)*   Outside USA

5. Which exciting country were you born in?

6. In which state (including the District of Columbia) do you live? Select from the drop-down menu.

Alabama	Louisiana	Oklahoma
Alaska	Maine	Oregon
Arizona	Maryland	Pennsylvania
Arkansas	Massachusetts	Rhode Island
California	Michigan	South Carolina
Colorado	Minnesota	South Dakota
Connecticut	Mississippi	Tennessee
Delaware	Missouri	Texas
District of Columbia	Montana	Utah
Florida	Nebraska	Vermont
Georgia	Nevada	Virginia
Hawaii	New Hampshire	Washington
Idaho	New Jersey	West Virginia
Illinois	New Mexico	Wisconsin
Indiana	New York	Wyoming
Iowa	North Carolina	Other *(Exit survey)*
Kansas	North Dakota	
Kentucky	Ohio	

7. What is your biological sex?

   Woman   Man

8. Imagine an FDA-approved miracle potion has become available.
   If you sip it, your biological aging process could slow, potentially
   doubling your lifespan. Let's assume it works and has no adverse
   side effects. Ignoring how much it might cost, would you sip it?
   (Selection is randomized)

   Yes   No *(Skip to 11)*

9. Please explain why you would like to potentially live longer:

10. Did your explanation refer to one of the ideas below?
    If so, select it. *(Selection is randomized)* *(After answering, skip to 12)*
    "Biologically aging slower could help me to . . . "

    Have a colossal amount of sex

    Delay death

    Accomplish deeds that take a long time

    Accumulate more wealth

    Spend more time with family

    Become smarter

    Assist charitable causes

    A different excellent idea (share your thoughts) _____

11. Please explain, in detail, why you would not sip the potion:

12. Let's leave the fantasy realm. Out of the options below, which one would you like to have more of for your life's duration? *(Selection is randomized)*

Ability to inspire confidence

Charisma

Courage

Self-control

Dexterity

Greater intuition about people

Intelligence

Perseverance

Self-confidence

13. Take a moment to visualize your perfect day. What leisure or work activities would you do? "On my perfect day, I would . . . "

14. Imagine yourself snug in bed. During the past week, what got you up each day? Choose as many as you wish.
(Selection is randomized)

Needed coffee

Empty bladder

Hungry

Partner got me up

Had to get up for my job

Had to get kids ready for school

Had to earn money

Pet needed to be walked/fed

Had to get to the gym

Felt guilty over staying too long in bed

Brain was restless

Other (share your thoughts)

15. Imagine yourself standing before your bathroom mirror. How did you respond to your wake-up reflection last week? Choose as many as you wish. *(Selection is randomized)*

I look like Mom/Dad

Woo! Looking good

I look tired

Have I put on weight?

Gray hair/No hair/Bad hair

Clean face and teeth? Check

I know I'm younger

Wrinkles

Other (share your thoughts)

16. Which quote is wisest? *(Selection is randomized)*

"United we stand, divided we fall."

"There is nothing you cannot accomplish."

"This American system of ours . . . gives each and every one of us a great opportunity if we only seize it."

"Anyone who has never made a mistake has never tried anything new."

"Look out for Number One. If you don't, no one else will."

"Life's most persistent and urgent question is, 'What are you doing for others?'"

17. Share the wisest quote you have heard or read, or share your own piece of wisdom:

18. During the last month, did you work toward a goal you'd set for yourself? Choose one answer. *(Selection is randomized)*

Life was too hectic

I prefer to go with the flow *(Skip to 21)*

I find it tricky to define goals *(Skip to 21)*

I'm figuring out my next goal/s *(Skip to 21)*

I worked toward a goal/s *(Skip to 20)*

Other (share your thoughts) *(Skip to 21)*

19. In the last month, what circumstances most drained your time and energy?

20. Which goal/s did you work toward?

21. Looking back over the past year, how do you feel about these aspects of your life? 1 = Dreadful, 10 = Perfect

I treated people as I want to be treated

I improved my skills and knowledge

I eased up on self-criticism

I exercised and nourished my body with care

I allowed my inner-child to play

I felt supported by my family, friends, colleagues, and the government

I found locations where I could recharge and be myself

I felt loved in my relationships

I managed my money efficiently

22. Which of these four descriptions is most like your personality:
    1 = Most like me
    2 = Second closest
    3 = Third closest
    4 = Least like me
    (Selection is randomized)

    You are highly energetic, crave novelty and adventure, and love to travel

    You manage people (from employees to family) effectively, value traditions, are highly organized, and prefer predictability to unpredictability

    You are focused, logical and competitive, enjoy intellectual debates, and make decisions with ease

    You are empathic, emotionally expressive, trust your intuition, and have deep friendships

23. Share a tip on how you live a happier life:

24. In the U.S., do bad things happen to well-behaved people, and good things happen to badly-behaved people?

Yes

Partly agree

Neutral

Partly disagree

No

25. At social events, what do you usually ask strangers about? Choose as many as you wish. *(Selection is randomized)*

Their occupation

Their family

Their friends

Whether they are filthy rich

For advice

Other (share your thoughts)

26. During the past 12 months, who has been calling the shots in your life? Choose one: *(Selection is randomized)*

Partner/spouse

Boss

Bank

Mom

Dad

Society

Me

My kid/s

Other (share your thoughts)

27. During the past year, who has wielded the most power over Americans' daily lives? Choose one:

Agribusiness

Bankers

China

Corporations

Hollywood/Media

Landlords

Lawyers

Oil tycoons

Pharmaceutical companies

Police

Politicians

Religious leaders

Voters

Other (share your thoughts)

28. Do you work in the industry you chose, or does someone close to you, such as a partner, parent, or friend? *(Selection is randomized)*

   No   Yes

29. How does the powerful group you chose affect your life?

30. If you were president, how would you lead the country? Choose one:

   Toward a society where people finish life socially and economically equal *(Skip to 32)*

   Toward a society where people are born socially and economically equal *(Skip to 32)*

   Neither

31. If you were president, how you would run the country?

32. Visualize yourself in bed, ready to fall asleep. What are you looking forward to about tomorrow? "I am looking forward to . . ."

33. How naughty were you yesterday?

	NAUGHTY Did this	NICE Did not do this
Watched mediocre TV shows		
Dressed in black		
Drank 2 or more caffeinated drinks		
Smoked a cigarette		
Sipped 3 or more beverages containing alcohol		
Spent more than an hour with a stressful person		
Consumed more calories than I burned		

34. Which answer best reflects your economic circumstances? Choose one: *(Selection is randomized)*

I'm unconcerned about my finances

In the last 6 months, I've spent money on luxury items, such as a vacation, designer clothing, or fine dining

I can only afford necessities

I have over $10,000 in credit card debt

Finances keep me awake at night

35. Have you put a ring on it?

Never married

Married/Civil union *(Skip to 37)*

Separated/Divorced/Widowed *(Skip to 38)*

36. You answered you've never been married.
Which best describes your relationship status?

Single and not actively dating *(Skip to 40)*

Would like to date *(Skip to 40)*

Dating several people *(Skip to 40)*

Dating one person—not going steady *(Skip to 40)*

Going steady *(Skip to 40)*

Cohabiting *(Skip to 39)*

37. You answered you are married/in a civil union, which best
describes your relationship status? *(After answering, skip to 39)*

First marriage

Second marriage (or more)

Civil union

Second civil union (or more)

38. You answered you are separated, divorced, or widowed. Which best describes your relationship status?

Single and not actively dating *(Skip to 40)*

Would like to date *(Skip to 40)*

Dating several people *(Skip to 40)*

Dating one person—not going steady *(Skip to 40)*

Going steady *(Skip to 40)*

Cohabiting

39. In your home, who typically makes these decisions?

	I Do	My Partner	It's Shared
What we eat for dinner			
What we do on the weekend			
When to interrupt a conversation			

40. Describe your employment situation. Choose one:

Retired

Employed for wages, full-time

Employed for wages, part-time

Employed for wages, two or more jobs

Homemaker

Temporarily exited work, seeking a position

Temporarily exited work, not seeking a position

Self-employed/freelancer

Student

Unable to work

41. Are you a homeowner?

No *(Skip to 43)*   Yes

42. Which of the following best describes your mortgage status?

Home has a mortgage/loan

Home is in negative equity

Home is "free and clear"

43. Are you currently or have you been a parent?

No *(Skip to 45)*   Yes

44. Which of the following best describes the flow of money between you and your child/children? Choose one:

I give money to my child/children

I don't give money to my child/children

I receive money from my child/children

45. Whose ECONOMIC policies do you tend to agree with?

Conservative Republicans

Moderate Republicans

Liberal Republicans

Conservative Democrats

Moderate Democrats

Liberal Democrats

Other group

Disinterested in politics

Don't know

Prefer not to answer

46. Whose SOCIAL policies do you tend to agree with?

Conservative Republicans

Moderate Republicans

Liberal Republicans

Conservative Democrats

Moderate Democrats

Liberal Democrats

Other group

Disinterested in politics

Don't know

Prefer not to answer

47. Describe your religious beliefs. Choose one:

God created Earth but is now unresponsive to prayers, does not perform miracles, and does not intervene in wars

Believe in one God who is involved with human affairs on Earth

Believe in Gods who are involved with human affairs on Earth

I don't believe a God or gods created Earth

Other (share your thoughts)

Prefer not to answer

Please accept this heartfelt thank-you
for sharing your wisdom.

"Show Me the Money" Question Guide

*"If you would know the value of money,
go and try to borrow some."*

—Benjamin Franklin

This mischievous survey invites you to share your wisdom about money.
(Questions 1 to 7 have been omitted; they were identical to the corresponding questions in "Seize the Day.")

8. A corporation wants to give you money. To get it, you must be medically unconscious for 12 months. Nothing sinister would happen to you in that time. If you decided the amount you'd receive, would you accept? *(Selection is randomized)*

    I might accept   I would not accept *(Skip to 10)*

9. How much cash would you want in exchange for being unconscious for a year?

    Enter the amount you'd want:
    $_____ *(After answering, skip to 11)*

10. Please explain why you did not accept the offer:

11. In a grocery store checkout line, the person behind taps your shoulder and asks, "In life, what's the best way to get money: borrow it, earn it, inherit it, marry it, or win it?" "The answer," you say, "is to . . . " *(Selection is randomized)*

Borrow it

Inherit it

Earn it

Marry it

Win it

12. Imagine you are a high-school career counselor. Which career would you recommend to students who live in the same state as you? Your recommendation should encourage skills growth and a livable income.

13. Do you know someone who works, or who has worked in the career you recommended?

Yes   No *(Skip to 15)*

14. Who works or has worked in that field?
   Choose as many as you wish.

   Me

   My romantic partner/spouse

   Mom

   Dad

   Friend

   Neighbor

   Sibling

   Other person

15. An independent single woman in her 20s seeks a lifetime of financial gain. Which career strategy should she take up? P.S. She is not about to win the lottery or inherit money. *(Selection is randomized)*

Hard work, determination, and avoidance of debt

Present an energetic professional attitude

Marry for money

Record a sex tape

Work outside the U.S.

Become a white-collar criminal

Be her own boss

Love what she does

Get academic qualifications

Invest in the stock market

Other (share your thoughts)

16. Which career strategy should an independent single man in his 20s take up? *(Selection is randomized)*

Hard work, determination, and avoidance of debt

Present an energetic professional attitude

Marry for money

Record a sex tape

Work outside the U.S.

Become a white-collar criminal

Be his own boss

Love what he does

Get academic qualifications

Invest in the stock market

Other (share your thoughts)

17. During the previous 12 months, think about the amount of money you've spent on your lifestyle. To be more content, how much extra money would you like per month (tax-free)? If additional money will not make you more content, type 0. *(If type "0," skip to 19)*

"Dear Money Genie,

Please deposit an additional $_____ per month into my bank account. Thank you."

18. Within the next 12 months, do you believe you can increase your monthly income by the amount you asked for?

No way

Not very believable

Somewhat believe

Believable

Absolutely

19. Which phrase best completes the following sentence?
"Having lots of money is awesome because you can . . . "
(Selection is randomized)

Buy whatever you desire

Cease to worry

Help others and donate to charity

Employ assistants

Keep studying and learning

Have sex with desirable people

Receive respect

Travel

Other (share your thoughts)

20. Complete the sentence again, this time with a naughty answer:
"Having lots of money is awesome because you can . . . "
(Selection is randomized)

Tell your boss to stick it

Tell someone in your family to cram it

Gloat at your high-school reunion

Make your ex realize losing you was the biggest
mistake of their life

Erect a moat and drawbridge to keep riff-raff out of your home

Other (share your thoughts)

21. Compared to 1980, which issues are better now?

	Better now	Better in the 1980s
Access to affordable medical care		
Ability to buy a comfortable home		
Pleasure obtained from driving		
Neighborhood safety		
Retirement benefits		

22. When it comes to managing your personal finances, how savvy do you feel? *(Individuals choosing "in-between", "somewhat struggling" or "struggling", skip to 24)*

Struggling

Somewhat struggling

In-between

Somewhat savvy

Savvy

23. Share a financial tip on how people can improve their lives without spending a fortune:

24. Take a moment to think about the American Dream of recent U.S. legal permanent residents. What kind of home do you think they want? *(Selection is randomized)*

White picket fence

Private island

Penthouse

Beach house

Brownstone

Ranch

Other (share your thoughts)

25. What kind of transport do you think new legal permanent residents want? *(Selection is randomized)*

    Motorbike

    SUV

    Private plane

    Nice shoes

    Hybrid

    Sports car

    Other (share your thoughts)

26. What do you think new legal permanent residents most want in their hands? *(Selection is randomized)*

    Shopping bags

    TV remote

    Smartphone

    Steering wheel

    Credit card

    Soul mate

    Other (share your thoughts)

27. What do you think new legal permanent residents most enjoy eating? *(Selection is randomized)*

Big Mac

Surf and turf

Pizza

Organic food

Other (share your thoughts)

28. Out of the people who became legal permanent residents last year, what percentage will fulfill their American Dream?

29. Is your personal American Dream the same as the dream you just described?

My dream is the same *(Skip to 31)*

My dream is different

I don't have an American Dream *(Skip to 31)*

30. Describe your American Dream:

31. During the last six months, have you noticed an item in somebody's possession you would like to own?

Oh, yes!

I have not seen anything I fancy *(Skip to 36)*

I have everything I want *(Skip to 36)*

32. Describe this delightful item:

33. Was the person with this item non-family or family?

Non-family

Family *(Skip to 35)*

34. Who had the item? *(After answering, skip to 36)*

Best friend

Friend

Neighbor

Boyfriend

Girlfriend

Stranger—man

Stranger—woman

Boss

Work colleague

Celebrity—man

Celebrity—woman

Other non-family

35. Who had the item?

My kid

Brother

Sister

Mom

Dad

Stepmom

Stepdad

Grandparent

My partner

Partner's brother

Partner's sister

Partner's parents

Other family member

36. Describe your employment situation. Choose one:

Retired *(Skip to 46)*

Employed for wages, full-time

Employed for wages, part-time

Employed for wages, two or more jobs *(Skip to 46)*

Homemaker *(Skip to 46)*

Temporarily exited work, seeking a position *(Skip to 46)*

Temporarily exited work, not seeking a position *(Skip to 46)*

Self-employed/freelancer *(Skip to 46)*

Student *(Skip to 46)*

Unable to work *(Skip to 46)*

37. How do you feel about your job? *(Selection is randomized)*

I enjoy my job *(Skip to 39)*

I do it for the money *(Skip to 39)*

It's okay *(Skip to 39)*

I want to stay in my profession but change jobs

I want to change my profession *(Skip to 39)*

Other (share your thoughts) *(Skip to 39)*

38. What is your main motivation for wanting to change jobs?
    (Selection is randomized)

    I want to work for a more successful company

    I want a promotion

    I want a better work-life balance

    I want more money

    I want to be treated with more respect

39. In your current job, have the following occurred?
    (If "Yes," skip to 42)

	Yes	No	Not to my knowledge
A coworker was close to burning out			
A coworker lied on their resume			
The company was breaking the law			

40. How would you respond if these events occurred at
    your current job? *(If "would intervene," "probably intervene,"
    or "probably not intervene," skip to 42)*

	I would intervene	Probably intervene	Probably not intervene	Not intervene
A coworker was close to burning out				
A coworker lied on their resume				
The company was breaking the law				

41. Explain why in your current job, you would not intervene:

42. In the last 12 months, have you turned down an offer of
    additional responsibility at your job?

    I turned down an offer of more responsibility

    I accepted an offer to take on more responsibility *(Skip to 44)*

    I did not receive such an offer *(Skip to 45)*

43. Why did you turn down the offer? Choose as many as you wish.
    (Next, skip to 45)

    I would have had less free time

    I would have had to relocate

    I would have had more stress

    I would have had to layoff workers

    There would have been more office politics

    Other (share your thoughts)

44. By accepting additional responsibility, what happened to you? Choose as many as you wish.

	Improved	Worsened	The Same
Mental stress levels			
Physical health			
Personal relationships			
Finances			
Office politics			
Hours worked			

45. Have these ever happened to you (on purpose or by accident)?

	Yes	No	Not applicable
Tried to pay lower taxes than you were supposed to			
Made a colleague cry			
Put work before family			
Put work before your physical/ mental health			
Worked for someone you did not respect			
You were disrespected in a workplace			

46. When a person asks, "What do you do for a living?" how do you feel as you answer?

Happy

Ashamed

Victorious

Resentful

Uncomfortable

Other (share your thoughts)

47. When a woman enters into a marriage or a civil union, which is better: for her partner to have money, or for her partner to love her? *(Only women see this question: men, skip to 50)*

For her partner to love her

For her partner to love her and to have money

For her partner to have money

48. Why did you choose your answer? *(Only women see this; then, skip to 52)*

49. When a man enters into a marriage or a civil union, which is better: for his partner to have money, or for his partner to love him? *(Only men see this)*

For his partner to love him

For his partner to love him and to have money

For his partner to have money

50. Why did you choose your answer? *(Only men see this)*

In this survey, the remaining questions matched qns. 34–38 and qns. 41–47 in "Seize the Day." However, married/civil union respondents who took this survey were also asked: "How worried are you that your partner might leave you for someone with more money?"

Not worried

A little worried

Neutral

Very worried

Extremely worried

Thank you for reading *Are You Buying This?*

Please review this book on Amazon.com, and/or tell your friends about it, so more folks can discover for themselves what Americans really think about money and life.

Wishing you every happiness,
J. J. Robertson

J. J. Robertson, a.k.a., the Brain Sucker®, has headed account-planning departments at award-winning U.S. ad agencies. She's presented research to Fortune 500 CEOs and has inspired top creative minds with her consumer insights. Robertson holds social science master's degrees from UCLA and the University of Edinburgh. She lives in Virginia, where she excels as a tea drinker.